# The World
## — OF THE —
# BABY

# The World
## OF THE
# BABY

*A celebration of infancy through the ages*

## Georgina O'Hara

Doubleday

New York London Toronto Sydney Auckland

Published by Doubleday
a division of Bantam Doubleday Dell Publishing Group, Inc.,
666 Fifth Avenue, New York, New York 10103

**Doubleday** and the portrayal of an anchor with a dolphin are
trademarks of Doubleday, a division of Bantam Doubleday Dell
Publishing Group, Inc.

LIBRARY OF CONGRESS
Library of Congress Cataloging-in-Publication Data

O'Hara, Georgina.
   The world of the baby/Georgina O'Hara. — 1st ed.
   p. cm.
   ISBN 0-385-26056-3
   1. Infants—History. 2. Infants' supplies—History. I. Title.
HQ774.033 1989
305.2′32—dc19
                                       88-25633
                                        CIP

ISBN 0–385–26056–3

First published in Great Britain by Michael Joseph, Ltd. 1989

Printed in Hong Kong
May 1989
First American Edition

Acknowledgements

The author and publisher are grateful to the following for permission to reproduce quoted material:
page 77 Mothercare Ltd; page 73 *Costume for Births, Marriages and Deaths*, by Phyllis Cunnington and
Catherine Lucas, A & C Black Ltd, 1972; pages 111, 143, 162, 168, *Nursery World*; page 77 *American
Baby*; page 187 the Literary Trustees of Walter de la Mare and The Society of Authors as their
representative; page 101 D. J. Enright, 'On the Death of a Child', *Collected Poems*, Oxford University
Press, 1981 and Watson, Little Ltd, licensing agents; pages 158, 176, 177 *The Lady*; page 70 Ogden
Nash 'Reflection on Babies', *I Wouldn't Have Missed It*, André Deutsch Ltd; page 73 *Royal Children* by
Celia Clear, Weidenfeld & Nicolson Ltd; page 76 *The Mother to Mother Baby Care Book* by Barbara Sills
and Jeanne Henry, Camaro Publishing Co.

*Title page*

*Early nineteenth-century view of rustic bliss by Charles Brocky*
*(1807–55)*

# Contents

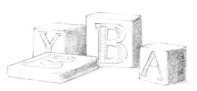

# Introduction

WHEN I began the research for this book, I expected to find that most of the historical literature on infancy would date from the nineteenth century, while the real wealth of information would come from the post-Spock years of this century. I imagined that in reviewing the years from the fourteenth century to around 1800 there would be scanty references to childbirth and the raising of children, and that infancy would be ignored altogether.

I was both right and wrong. While there were indeed books, pamphlets and essays published on childbirth – some authors seemed to have used little else but their imaginations to write them, others were quite far advanced in their thinking – they would have been available to the relatively few. One of the most famous books, at least the one most often cited by historians, was *An Essay upon Nursing, and the Management of Children from Their Birth to Three Years of Age*, written by Dr William Cadogan and published fairly recently in our history in 1748.

It is important to remember that in the centuries before television, there was an enormous time lag between the presentation of an idea and its acceptance. Ideas that we now consider obsolete took years to be accepted, as they were passed on by word of mouth from mother to daughter. There were no such things as ante-natal clinics where women could obtain medical information about themselves and their babies. Today we have easy access to books overflowing with information for the mother and her child. These are manuals, instructive, caring and reassuring to the parents, and much of the mystique of childbirth is now neatly packaged between 250 pages.

But for the mother living in Roman Britain, or in the early years of the sixteenth century, for example, such advice was not readily available. No doubt she would consult other female members of her own family, which would inevitably result in children being brought up in much the same manner for years as information, rather like old clothing, was passed down from one generation to the next.

In looking at the history of infants I came to understand that by twentieth-century sensibilities babies in the past were shockingly mistreated. If you were, for example, a mother in the Middle Ages, you would most likely have an unwashed baby. Back then, people believed that water was contaminated and they wouldn't drink it or wash in it for fear of contracting one of the many diseases that were prevalent at the time. You would have an unwashed child, not because you were lazy, but simply because you subscribed to the common beliefs of your time. That your child might suffer because of your views probably never occurred to you. Germ theory was at least four hundred years away. Sickness and death were blamed on the devil or the Evil Eye or, depending where you lived, river spirits or mountain gods.

One of the most interesting things that I discovered in writing this book was that although our increasing awareness of social history inevitably includes childhood, not much attention has been paid to infancy. Most museums have a number of infant garments – shifts, dresses, caps and christening robes – but few other items have been collected. It is understandable in a way because little has survived the centuries, but what exists today lies, in many instances, undocumented, unphotographed, almost unloved one could say, in boxes on shelves, and rarely seen by the public. Museums, of course, are hindered by financial considerations but there is an argument for more to be said and done on the subject of infancy and our attitudes, past and present, towards it. After all, without successfully negotiating infancy, a human being is unable to embark on childhood.

It is difficult for us to accept the callousness and indifference with which babies were treated in the past. Rich and poor alike fed their infants in the same manner, so to be born into a wealthy household was not necessarily a guarantee of survival. It is important to recognize that despite concerted efforts by those who cared, babies in the past died in large numbers and many children never reached the age of ten. A woman in the nineteenth century might have given birth to ten children during her lifetime, of whom only four

*Dutch Interior with Mother and Children by nineteenth-century painter Bernard Posthast*

would have survived childhood. What appears, with hindsight, to be gross negligence was really ignorance and helplessness to be able to do anything in the face of illness.

Without contraception, many women could expect to be pregnant almost every two years and while some births must have been welcomed, others must have been dreaded. Until this century childbirth was viewed with enormous fear. Childbirth, similar to most things that people did not understand, had strong associations with witchcraft. Many women did not survive the birth of a child and large numbers of those who were fortunate enough to see their newborn died of complications shortly afterwards. If the man-midwife, as he was known, with his hooks and knives, intervened during labour a woman might be required to spend the rest of her life as a semi-invalid.

If mother survived there was no guarantee that her child would be able to do the same. Infant feeding practices in the past were usually a matter of life or death. Children were fed on a hopelessly inadequate diet which resulted in vitamin deficiencies, illness and, quite often, death.

The medical history of childbirth practices and infancy makes sombre reading. The choices we have today, of hi-tech, instrument-dominated births or more 'natural' deliveries, both of which have become part of our culture, were non-existent until relatively few years ago. Caesarean sections were carried out in the Middle Ages but the success rate would have been minimal given the lack of familiarity with hygiene and the surgical procedures at the time. Leeches were used by doctors who hoped to cure all kinds of ailments, along with compounds of mercury, herbal teas, garlic – which was thought to cure whooping cough – and opiates to quieten noisy babies. Inoculations were used in the eighteenth century, but it was 1891 before an anti-serum was discovered for diphtheria, and 1907 before meningitis could be treated. Ante-natal care was not available until the first part of this century and post-natal depression was not acknowledged by the medical world until the 1920s.

During the eighteenth century there was a public awakening to the plight of infants. By the nineteenth century this concern by the middle and upper classes had made babies the objects of strange ideas. One writer felt that adults, who gave off strange gases through the pores of their skin, would do well to stay away from babies. Many Victorians viewed infants as essentially evil creatures that needed to be firmly disciplined. Cuddling, in many cases, was frowned upon. Considering the odds, it amazes me to think that people were able to survive in such numbers, and I continue to marvel at the resilience of babies in the hands of their parents.

We humans are fascinated with ourselves, our origins, how we think and feel; and yet until fairly recently the most basic social group, that of the family, into which most children are born, has been largely disregarded by social historians. It is the familial setting – be that single- or many-parented – that provides the arena for infancy, the parents, siblings, relatives and friends supplying the artefacts and objects of infancy. In nudging the family to one side we have overlooked the first state of our lives after birth.

No book can expect to truly know all there is about infancy over thousands of years. Toys and rattles cannot speak to us of the babies who played with them, cribs cannot recite the lullabies to which they were rocked. The women who could have told us how they felt were not able to write, or, if they could write, they lived at a time when it was not popular practice to analyse and verbalize one's emotions.

So much of infancy is lost to us: objects outgrown and discarded, one set of ideas abandoned for another. But adults find great pleasure in miniature things, particularly those that remind them, on a subconscious level perhaps, of their own childhoods. Infancy one does not remember. But everyone associates it with a time of helplessness, a time when things were done for one, a time of protection, a brief world which bears little resemblance to the harsh realities of the one in which we grow up. Infant objects, such as shoes, coats, bonnets and bibs, invoke a kind of nostalgia, a yearning for the time one has no hope of recalling. Rattles, pacifiers and soft, woolly teddies reflect images of a small world, a lost world, a world we once held in our arms.

In a nuclear age, where the population is declining in some parts of the world, interest in childhood, and therefore infancy, is stronger than ever. Babies are more visible, even, one could argue, more socially acceptable. By studying over the centuries how people treated their young, how they dressed them, what they fed them, where they were laid to sleep and how society felt about them, a fascinating picture has emerged – albeit one taken from adulthood and hindsight – of that brief time at the beginning of a human life.

At first the infant,
Mewling and puking in the nurse's
arms.

*As You Like It,* William Shakespeare

# BEGINNINGS

# Signs of Life

A book that looks at the marvellous, curious and multifarious ways in which we have treated infancy in the past must start necessarily with conception. The desire for children in most cultures is the desire to carry on the family name, the extreme of this being the necessity for a king to produce a male heir in countries where a queen is unable to rule. But children fulfil other functions in a family than being its heirs. A child can grow up to run the family business, fight for valuable land, or plant the next crop which will feed not only himself but the ageing parents who gave birth to him. In some countries, such as famine-starved Ethiopia, the more children the parents have the more comfortable and secure they feel about their old age.

Fertility associations are entrenched in every culture, from prehistoric times onwards. Today, the origins have been lost and the meanings are less significant, but we continue to uphold the traditions. This is most evident at weddings when the plant baby's breath, symbolizing fertility, is used in a bride's bouquet, and when confetti and rice are thrown at the newly wed couple, replacing the traditional nuts and seeds of long ago. Although the origins have been lost to history, as so many traditions, old shoes, which are curiously enough thought to be symbolic of the female sex organs, are believed to signify many children, and in England they are tied to the rear of the car in which the bride and bridegroom leave the wedding party. This gives an altogether different meaning to the fairytale of *Cinderella*.

An ear of corn is another emblem of fertility as it symbolizes the idea of germination and growth. Life in the past was associated with the crops and with the harvests, and it is from these aspects of daily life that so many symbols are taken.

Every culture has a number of fertility rites embedded within it, and the beliefs and superstitions connected with these rites are expressions of hope. Some of the ideas concerning fertility are common to women who live at opposite ends of the globe. In Europe in the Middle Ages, for example, a woman who wanted to get pregnant would drink the water in which the village blacksmith had placed his tongs to cool. In the East, women have been known to drink the water in which metal workers had washed their hands. Historically there has always been a close association between alchemy and metallurgy which might account for these practices which, bizarre as they

LIB. 25.    *Of Monsters and Prodigies.*    655

*The picture of Dorothie, great with childe with manie children.*

*Martin Cromerus* the autor of the Polish histo- rie, writeth that one *Margaret*, a woman sprung from a noble and ancient familie neer *Cracovia*, and wife to Count *Virboslaus*, brought forth at one birth thirtie five live children, upon the twentieth daie of *Jan.* in the year 1296. *Franciscus Picus Mirandula* writeth that one *Dorothie* an Italian had twentie children at two births; at the first nine, and at the second eleven, and that shee was so big, that shee was forced to bear up her bellie, which laie upon her knees, with a broad and large scarf tied about her neck, as you may see by this figure. *The ninth Book of the Polish Histo-rie.*

"DOROTHIE, GREAT WITH CHILDE WITH MANIE CHILDREN"

THE LASS OF LYNN'S
SORROWFUL LAMENTATION
FOR THE LOSS OF HER
MAIDENHEAD

I am a young Lass of *Lynn*
Who often said thank you too.
My Belly's now almost to my
    chin
    I cannot tell what to do.

My being so free and so kind
Does make my heart to rue
The sad effects of this I find
    I cannot tell what to do.

My Petticoats which I wore
And likewise my Aprons too
Alass! they are all too short
    before
    I cannot tell what to do . . .

A cradle I must provide
A chair and possett too
Nay! likewise twenty things
    beside
    I cannot tell what to do . . .

I came as of good a Race
As most in Lynn's fair Town
And cost a great deal bringing-
    up
But a little Thing laid me down.

                        Anon

may seem to us, certainly continued right up to the nineteenth century and perhaps even beyond, in both parts of the world.

In some corners of the world, getting pregnant is a far more complex and time-consuming affair than we would assume. Several African tribes reject the idea that conception can be the result of a few moments of passion, believing instead that the baby is formed by prolonged sexual intercourse over a period of weeks. These concepts are usually found in societies that place strong emphasis on the role spirits have in procreation. Spirits are thought to be an essential part of conception. They must accompany sexual intercourse, because although the male and female can create the body of a child, a spirit is needed to give it a soul.

The idea of spirit babies stretches from one end of the globe to the other. The American Hidatsa Indians thought infant souls lived in 'baby hills'. Their women would leave toys at the foot of the hills, trying to persuade the babies to descend and come into their homes. Eskimos believed that the souls of children waited on top of the snow and a woman who passed by with her boot laces undone would become pregnant if the spirits jumped inside her boots.

Other American Indian tribes believed that the souls of babies lived in trees, or in special stones which were just waiting for a young woman to pass by so that her body could be invaded. Barren women, or those who wanted a child, would therefore visit rocky places and walk under the branches of trees in the hopes of catching an invisible baby soul. There still exists also the belief that although the woman forms the child, it is the man who gives the baby its spiritual soul, and he is the one who is congratulated by the rest of the tribe for bringing a healthy child into the world.

Before people understood their bodies as well as we do today, menstruation and the emission of bodily fluids were greatly feared. Menstruating women were isolated in numerous societies, and in some instances this practice continues today. It was a common thought amongst medieval men that each time they had intercourse they were shortening their lives; this idea persists today in the most unlikely parts of the world although it seems to have no effect whatsoever on the frequency of sexual activity. In India, tiny children were thought to exist in sperm. Up until the seventeenth century it was a common belief in France that both men and women contributed seed at the moment of conception. A few African tribes think that conception occurs only when menstrual blood is mixed with semen.

Edward VI as a Child, *by Hans Holbein the Younger c. 1538. Male heirs were essential to every family and especially Royal families. Edward VI was the son of Henry VIII and Jane Seymour. He succeeded his father at the age of nine but died seven years later*

PARVVLE PATRISSA, PATRIÆ VIRTVTIS ET HÆRES
ESTO, NIHIL MAIVS MAXIMVS ORBIS HABET.
GNATVM VIX POSSVNT COELVM ET NATVRA DEDISSE,
HVIVS QVEM PATRIS, VICTVS HONORET HONOS.
ÆQVATO TANTVM, TANTI TV FACTA PARENTIS,
VOTA HOMINVM, VIX QVO PROGREDIANTVR, HABENT
VINCITO, VICISTI, QVOT REGES PRISCVS ADORAT
ORBIS, NEC TE QVI VINCERE POSSIT, ERIT.

17

She had never wholly cared for him, she did not at all care for him now. She had dreaded him, winced before him, succumbed to adroit advantages he took of her helplessness; then, temporarily blinded by his ardent manners, had been stirred to confused surrender awhile: had suddenly despised and disliked him, and had run away. That was all. Hate him she did not quite; but he was dust and ashes to her, and even for her name's sake she scarcely wished to marry him.

'You ought to have been more careful if you didn't mean to get him to make you his wife!'

'O mother, my mother!' cried the agonized girl, turning passionately upon her parent as if her poor heart would break. 'How could I be expected to know? I was a child when I left this house four months ago. Why didn't you tell me there was danger in menfolk? Why didn't you warn me? Ladies know what to fend hands against, because they read novels that tell them of these tricks; but I never had the chance o' learning in that way, and you did not help me!'

Her mother was subdued.

'I thought if I spoke of his fond feelings and what they might lead to, you would be hontish wi' him and lose your chance,' she murmured, wiping her eyes with her apron. 'Well, we must make the best of it, I suppose. 'Tis nater, after all, and what do please God!'

*Tess of the D'Urbervilles,* Thomas Hardy

Because of their fruit-bearing capabilities, and the symbolism of regeneration, which is of great significance to the Chinese, trees have played an important part in the history of fertility rites, particularly in Eastern European and Russian folk cosmology. In Yugoslavia they were the object of a fertility rite in which a women would put her chemise over a fruit-bearing tree on the night before St George's Day. The following morning she would take it off the tree and put it on herself, hoping to transfer some of the tree's powers to herself.

In Roman times women gathered under the wild fig tree to honour Juno, the goddess of women, where they would engage in a mock fight, beating the fertility into each other. In northern India women went to a sacred palm and picked a coconut. In other parts of the world women were known to roll on the ground beneath an apple tree, hoping to soak up its powerful properties.

Nuts and seeds have strong fertility associations, especially in England where, even in the early twentieth century, a girl who went 'nutting' – collecting the nuts that fall from trees in the autumn – would not go out on

Sunday in her special nutting dress made with a bag in the front. This was in case the devil climbed inside her bag, which would mean that she would be pregnant when she married. The hazelnut has particular significance as a fertility symbol. The pomegranate, the seeds of which were believed by the Greeks to have sprung from the blood of Dionysus, the god of life-forces, is thought to be lucky in bringing children, as are rice and nuts, which is why rice is thrown at weddings.

Ancient Greeks made love in a freshly ploughed field. In nature the earth is female and the plough is therefore a symbol of fertility also. The Greek goddess Eileithyia, or Artemis, who is often depicted kneeling or giving birth, was the recipient of many honey cakes, wine, incense and oil at her temple altars. Egyptian women who wanted children prayed to an effigy of a large hippopotamus that had numerous breasts. The hippopotamus represents strength which to Egyptians was related to ideas of fertility and motherhood. Water also had fertility associations: another reason why the hippopotamus, who spends a great deal of time in the water, was an appropriate symbol.

Mistletoe is a parasitic plant which was used by the Druids, although its origins have not been traced. It is often found entwined on the branches of an oak tree and it symbolizes regeneration. Mistletoe was a medieval cure for sterility, and newly married women carried it with them. If they wanted a child they would also drink a brew which was made from the first wild cornflowers that appeared in the fields. In the Middle Ages a couple wanting to conceive would have to make sure that all the doors in the house were firmly closed and that none of the locks were unsecured. On their wedding nights young women would place garlic in the keyhole of the door – but this might have had more to do with peeping Toms than anything else. Communal baths, especially those taken at the medieval spa of Baden, were highly recommended for women who wanted to become pregnant, although no evidence survives which could indicate whether or not it was the water or the proximity of men and women to each other which led to the success rate.

Other things were eaten, drunk or dug up to increase one's chances of pregnancy. Crabs, lobsters and prawns are still favoured in some parts of the world as aids to fertility. Eating nutmeg apparently had its advantages, although nothing has been proved, as did sitting over hot fumes of catmint, or sipping a drink made from the peony. Walapai Indians cut off the feet of gophers which they boiled and then ate. Right through the Middle Ages

'Plenty of nuts, plenty of cradles.'
Old English Saying

pregnancy was thought to be encouraged if a woman ate onions and eggs. It was suggested that men drank olive oil before intercourse. In Mexico, pregnancy was believed to be induced by boiling fresh pine resin, with three roots from a corn plant, which was then drunk while it was still hot. Alternatively one could make a brew from the sage plant. The poisonous mandrake root, used by the ancient Hebrews and Babylonians as an aphrodisiac and aid against barrenness, was still being dug up in the seventeenth century. Snakes have been used as fertility symbols in the past. The snake is a symbol of energy and strength, and ultimately of destruction. It symbolizes seduction but it is also associated with rebirth in the way it sheds its skin. In fifteenth-century Italy cherries were popular symbols, while German and Scandinavian folk traditions associated the stork with birth. For one of the most popular symbols of birth, there is very little known about the stork. Dedicated to the goddess Juno by the Romans, the stork was a symbol of piety and of the traveller, hence the expression still in use today of the stork bringing the baby.

If all else failed one could always walk in the shadow of a strong, fertile woman who was thought to be able to transfer her fertile powers to the woman behind her.

Once pregnant, a woman in almost every culture must observe certain rules. Until recent times she would be expected to play a very passive role, and in many cases she would be hidden from the view of the rest of the world. Subjected to suspicion during pregnancy and isolation during labour, she would be allowed to return to her community, symbolically and literally, only after she had been ritually cleansed or after a 'churching'. The word 'pregnant' was never mentioned in thousands of Victorian families; people referred instead to a woman being in a 'delicate condition'. In the days when feminine modesty prevented a woman from being able to discuss frankly her condition with a doctor, she might, instead, indicate on an anatomical doll, designed for the purpose, exactly what her ailments were and where they were located.

In the past there was no such thing as classes to prepare a woman and her partner for childbirth, or visits to the doctor who would examine the mother-to-be. Roman women prayed to the goddess Prosa for the foetus to be placed in the correct position for an easy delivery, and to the goddess Postverta for a safe and happy confinement. In the seventeenth century a woman might be bled, using leeches two or three times during her pregnancy.

## THE MAID'S LONGING

A maiden of late
Whose name was Sweet Kate,
She dwelt in London near Aldersgate;
　Now list to my ditty, declare it I can,
　She would have a child without help
　　of a man.

To a doctor she came,
A man of great fame,
Whose deep skill in physick report did
　proclaim.
　Quoth she: 'Mr Doctor, shew me if
　　you can
　How I may conceive without help
　　of a man.'

'Then listen,' quoth he,
'Since it must be,
This wondrous strange med'cine
　I'll shew presently;
　Take nine pound of thunder, six legs
　　of a swan,
　And you shall conceive without help
　　of a man.

'The love of false harlots,
The faith of false varlets,
With the truth of decoys that walk in
　their scarlet,
　And the feathers of a lobster,
　　well fry'd in a pan,

And you shall conceive without help
　of a man.

'Nine drops of rain
Brought hither from Spain,
With the blast of a bellows quite over
　the main,
　With eight quarts of brimstone
　　brew'd in a can,
　And you shall conceive without help
　　of a man.

'Six pottles of lard,
Squeez'd from rock hard,
With nine turkey eggs, each as long as a
　yard,
　With pudding of hailstones well
　　bak'd in a pan,
　And you shall conceive without help
　　of a man.

'These med'cines are good,
And approved have stood,
Well temper'd together with a pottle of
　blood
　Squeez'd from a grasshopper and the
　　nail of a swan,
　To make maids conceive without
　　help of a man.'

Morning sickness is unknown to women in some cultures, and those people who have studied them have not yet been able to trace why these women never appear to suffer from it. Those tribes that recognize morning sickness as a symptom of pregnancy consider it to be the result of the pregnant woman seeing her husband; that the sight of his clothes can bring about sickness is a popular belief.

Common to many corners of the world is the idea that if a woman should raise her arms above her head after the third month of pregnancy, she is running the risk of entwining the baby's umbilical cord about its neck. Superstitious nineteenth-century Pennsylvania-German settlers would not allow pregnant women to walk under a clothes line. American Indian women were not allowed to ride horses and they had to stay away from corpses. In other cultures, graveyards were taboo for pregnant women, and in some parts of America today horror movies are considered to be forbidden television viewing. In Ancient China pregnant women were carried about in sedan chairs which were draped with fishing nets to protect them from evil spirits. A list of other unacceptable practices during pregnancy includes: don't eat left overs, don't be too forthright or aggressive and don't gossip. The taboos extended to what women thought and they were encouraged to think peaceful thoughts in order to have a calm baby.

Certain foods were forbidden, such as intestines, eels, frogs, sago and coconuts which came from sacred places. Women were urged to stay away from crops as their seed was thought to compete with that growing beneath the earth. For this reason, also, they were advised not to dig in the ground. In the Middle Ages German monks allowed pregnant women to fish in their brooks on the condition that they kept one foot on land. Basket weaving was another occupation that was thought to be dangerous to pregnant women as it symbolized a difficult labour. Women who wanted a boy were urged not to cut anything in half until after the baby was born. Madame de Sévigné, writing to her daughter in 1676, felt that the loss of her daughter's child at eight months was due to her soaking her feet. She also commented that it was useless to hope that a child born prematurely at eight months would survive. Today, we urge pregnant women not to drink alcohol, although abstinence would have been impossible in past times when the drinking water carried more dangers than the alcohol.

Throughout history the birth of a boy was seen to be preferable to that of a girl, with the notable exception of the Romans who were, on the whole, favourably disposed towards women. As women, in many cases, were forbidden to inherit, the survival of the family name depended on the birth of a male. Kings have always needed sons to inherit their crowns. Henry VIII tried very hard to secure his lineage with male heirs, marrying six wives in the process. One set of parents were so hopeful of a son that they carried things to an extreme: Queen Mary I, who married Philip II of Spain in 1554, was desperate for a male heir. She had at least one phantom pregnancy, but perhaps the most famous one was when the royal couple actually informed Cardinal Pole in Rome that they had been blessed with a son. In fact, Mary wasn't pregnant at all but was suffering from dropsy.

Many people could not wait for the moment of birth to discover the sex of their child and they engaged in elaborate guesswork. From the Ancient Egyptians to the people who lived in Europe in the sixteenth and seventeenth centuries, the following method was popularly practised. In order for a woman to find out if she was having a boy or a girl, she would put wheat and barley, which had been mixed with dates and sand, into linen bags, over which she would urinate every day. If the wheat grew she would give birth to a boy. If the barley grew she would have a daughter. If neither wheat or barley grew then it was unlikely that her pregnancy would run to term.

The most common suggestion was that a woman who had a pronounced oval bump, carried high, during pregnancy would give birth to a girl, while a woman who carried her baby widely across her hips would have a boy. But the Bedouin tribes of the Middle East believe the opposite. In the twentieth century women dangle a wedding ring from a thread of cotton over their abdomens to see which way it circles. If it circles to the left it is thought that the baby will be a boy, to the right a girl. This is reversed, depending on where one lives.

For centuries many country people have lived by the waxing and waning of the moon. They believe that children, or animals, born under a full moon are stronger and likely to grow more quickly than those born under a waning, or decreasing, moon. They believe, also, that a boy born under a waning moon signifies that the next child will be a girl, and vice versa. On the other hand, a child born under a waxing, or growing, moon will be followed by a child of the same sex.

Since the moon's cycles are linked to astrology, there are certain times

ON OTHO

Three daughters Otho hath, his
    onely heirs,
But will by no means let them
    learn to write;
'Cause, after his own humour
    much he fears,
They'll one day learn, love-
    letters to indite.
The youngest now's with childe;
    who taught her then,
Or of her self learn'd she to hold
    her pen?

Anon

*Hans Holbein the Younger (1497–1543)*
*was one of the few artists to illustrate*
*pregnant women*

during the month when it is considered auspicious to sow seeds on the land; just as there are other times when the combination of the moon's cycle and the menstrual cycle can determine the sex of a child.

One of the age-old methods of discovering the sex of an unborn child is to divide in half the time between the last day of menstruation to the first day of the next period. If conception took place when the moon is in what are thought to be the 'masculine' signs of Aries, Gemini, Leo, Libra, Sagittarius or Aquarius, in the last half of a woman's menstrual cycle (except for the last seventy-two hours before menstruation starts again), the child is likely to be a boy. A child conceived in the last seventy-two hours of the menstrual cycle will be a girl. A baby girl will also be born if conception occurs in the first half of the menstrual cycle when the moon is in the 'feminine' signs of Taurus, Cancer, Virgo, Scorpio, Capricorn and Pisces. Today's hi-tech methods of discovering the sex of a child would astonish people from earlier centuries.

Astrology played an important role in the birth of a child. In China it has long been the custom for parents to consult an astrologer shortly after the birth in order to have the infant's horoscope 'cast'. By doing this the parents would be able to determine the child's future, ascertain his or her strong points and weaknesses and begin work on finding another child with a compatible horoscope who would make a suitable future husband or wife. The casting of a natal horoscope was popular amongst nobles in fifteenth- and sixteenth-century France and Italy when astrologers were appointed to the courts. These men also fulfilled roles as astronomers, alchemists and physicians but during the seventeenth century their popularity declined.

# An Ounce of Prevention

There have been, in all probability, far fewer women who have desired children and who have been unable to conceive them than there have been women who wish to prevent childbirth altogether. It should be remembered that the prevention of birth was just as important to some women in the past as it is to some women now. Too many children, born to impoverished families, made a simple equation: more mouths, less food. Some tribal cultures punished a woman if she had too many children. She was thought of as being over-sexed, and the size of her family meant that she became ostracized. Of course, the fathers of the children were excused from this treatment.

Many women in history have found themselves confronted with the task of raising a child on their own. The young girl employed as a servant in a large household who found herself unwilling, or unable, to refuse the advances of a man, might find herself not only pregnant but jobless. These women were shunned by society and they very often became destitute. In the hope of saving their children, and themselves, many attempted to conceal the birth. Once the child was born it was then left on a doorstep or taken to a hospital where the poor young mother hoped someone would take it in and bring it up for her.

The huge incidence of infanticide, particularly in the eighteenth century, attests to the problem of unwanted children, but right into the twentieth century, thinly disguised abortifacients were advertised in British national newspapers as pills to help 'women in all their ailments'.

Religious creeds put aside, which they often were, women, and sometimes men, have endeavoured to prevent pregnancy by a number of methods which to us today seem most bizarre.

The South African tribe, the Djuka, was quite advanced in its thinking about contraception, having deduced that sperm created babies and that therefore sperm needed to be trapped before it reached the uterus. Djuka women placed a vegetable-seed pod inside themselves to trap the sperm. Women of the Kasai Basin in Central Africa created a cervical 'plug' made of grass, while women from other tribes used roots, crushed and ground, for the same purpose. Women of Easter Island covered the uterine mouth with some kind of seaweed or algae. In Ancient Egypt, a lint tampon soaked in herbal liquid and honey was used, the liquid made from acacia tips which when allowed to ferment produce lactic acid, a spermicide. Other ancient contraceptives were soft wool moistened with oil or honey and placed at the uterine opening, or a cervical cap made from beeswax.

For many people, contraception was simply a matter of singing special songs, or asking the local witchdoctor to chant some magical words. Some of the Maori peoples believed that stones could make a woman infertile and therefore surrounded her with them.

The wearing of amulets was thought to be a reliable prevention against pregnancy, and amulets of mule's earwax were especially popular amongst Greeks and Romans. Asparagus juice was credited with special qualities; while in the Middle Ages, a drink of tea made from parsley and lavender was believed to be a safety precaution. Eating beans on an empty stomach before intercourse was yet another method. Perhaps, to us, the most intriguing idea of all was that of jumping backwards seven times after intercourse. It would be about as effective as holding your breath during your partner's orgasm. In the twentieth century some women believed that pregnancy could be prevented by coughing violently after sex to expel the semen. The most universal custom is that of tying knots around the house, or the person, and it has been suggested as the reason why young lovers would traditionally tie knots in their handkerchiefs, although today we think of the custom more as a reminder to ourselves not to forget something.

In some societies the man took responsibility and put vinegar on his penis. The withdrawal method was used but it was thought that if a man withdrew too quickly the woman's womb would catch a chill. In addition, the withdrawal method was thought to weaken the man. The condom was evidently in fairly wide use in Europe by the seventeenth century – condoms were known since Roman times – but it was usually associated with prostitution. Condoms, made of lint, linen rag or dried sheep gut, were employed during the Middle Ages as aids to prevent the spread of syphilis or 'the pox', which was prevalent at the time.

Abstinence will always be the most effective form of preventing pregnancy, and this is practised in a number of communities in the world, where couples are not allowed to have intercourse until their offspring learn how to walk.

# Superstitions

THERE is no other subject which has more folklore surrounding it than pregnancy and the subsequent birth of a child. The natural fears of pain during childbirth when there were no means by which to ease it, and the possibility of the death of either mother or child, resulted in one superstition in particular which can be found in just about every culture in the world. Long before the nineteenth century, when scientists discovered that germs were responsible for causing so many infant deaths, people attributed sudden illness and death to the Evil Eye. In primitive cultures this remains true today. The Evil Eye is an ancient concept of a malevolent mind which can project itself through the eyes of an individual, who brings misfortune, pain and death to the recipient of his gaze, most often a baby, a small child or a pregnant woman. Domestic animals, such as cows, sheep, chickens and pigs, are also affected, and the Eye is considered sufficiently powerful in some cultures to wipe out a whole family. For centuries, certain Mediterranean peoples believed the Evil Eye to be responsible for half the deaths in the world.

Anthropologists have found the Evil Eye concept in almost every culture across the globe. It is mentioned both in the Bible and the Talmud. The Romans described its workings as *fascinato*, from which our word 'fascinate' derives. To fascinate, in its true sense, means to hold prisoner by the power of a look, the most dramatic example being the captivating gaze of a snake. It may be connected with the fabulous mythical animal, the basilisk, a snake-like creature with a three-pointed crest and three-pointed tail. Medieval people believed that the glance of the basilisk could kill.

*This precious-looking gold and pink coral rattle has a coral gumstick at one end for a teething baby to chew upon and bells and a whistle at the other. It was made by Nicholas Roosevelt (1715–69)*

Other than the basilisk, women were considered to be the bearers of this peculiar ocular power. In some societies, menstruating women and women in childbirth were thought to be especially dangerous and they were isolated for that reason. In medieval times the Evil Eye was one of a witch's most feared powers. Few men have been credited with the Evil Eye.

In all societies, without exception, babies are thought to be the most susceptible to the Evil Eye. It was believed that the Eye could be projected unconsciously by a woman if she felt unacknowledged envy or jealousy towards the newborn baby or its mother. The danger was considered greatest in childbirth, when an envious glance from a woman attending the mother could carry misfortune to the child. The Bedouins smoke a rag of fabric under the nose of a woman who is having difficulty in labour. They reason that her pregnancy has gone well so far and thus attracted a great deal of envy. The fumes from the rag are intended to destroy the influence of the Evil Eye.

In countries as far apart as India and Mexico, women visiting a newborn baby and its mother will not look at the infant in case they inadvertently cast the Eye on the child. In the Philippines, the custom is to place crossed sticks at the baby's head to avert the danger. Words, not just looks, have been considered equally dangerous and in a great many cultures the newborn infant could not be praised, as this would be interpreted as envy. Any words of praise in Roman times would have to have been accompanied by the word *praefiscini*, meaning 'wishing no harm'.

Ancient Greeks placed olive leaves on the door and smeared pitch in the doorway of a house where a woman was giving birth, in order to prevent evil spirits from entering and to warn others away.

In some Eastern cultures the evil spirits are believed to appreciate beauty and, for that reason, infants are dressed in filthy clothes. Parents felt more secure in the knowledge that a child dressed in this manner was less likely to incite envy from other people. Traditionally, boys, who were more highly prized than girls, were dressed in girls' clothing in an attempt to trick the spirits.

Not a method of washing, but a preventive measure was the habit of spitting on a newborn child. Indeed, Ancient Greeks were known to spit on themselves to ward off the Evil Eye, but most often the ritual was reserved for babies. Medieval nurses licked the faces of their charges, while peasants all over the world spat in the faces of their children if they wanted to deflect the

gaze of the Eye. In rural parts of India, babies are rubbed with oil and then the mother spits on her fingers which she rubs on the baby's forehead for protection.

In the West we tend to think of the adornment of babies as having a purely decorative function, the bright colours and patterns pleasing both parent and child. But the elaborately stitched head ornaments worn, since man was able to fashion them, by babies from Palestine to Thailand; the intricate necklaces often found on infants in remote African tribal villages; and the anklets worn by baby girls in Nepal have far greater significance than expressions of a people's skill at the loom or with a needle. These items are amulets and, in many cases, they are still worn today as prevention against the effects of the Evil Eye.

Although many infant objects speak of the hopes, the desires and the aspirations of the parents, amulets – and amuletic symbols woven into clothes – are solely designed to ward off all manner of evil. To our eyes the designs seem to reflect the skill of the embroideress in selecting complimentary patterns and shapes, or the jeweller in his clever choice of metal and stone, when in fact the selection and configuration of shapes and symbols is a complex formula, which has, more often than not, been passed down from generation to generation.

Odd numbers are thought to have protective powers, and many signs and raised patterns are grouped together in threes or fives or sevens. These numbers are not reserved for mothers and babies but can be found in the way tribesmen group together their tents or the way in which women adorn their clothes. From the East come the crescent shape and the five-point star, both ancient signs to ward off evil. In Africa amber is used extensively for making amulets and jewellery. It is highly prized for what is considered to be its ability to protect the wearer from malevolent forces. In the Mediterranean the image of the fish, the ancient symbol of life and fertility, was used in decorative form in amulets. Today one can still find tiny silver fish on charm bracelets which are given as christening presents. In that part of the world, belief in the Evil Eye remains strong today, and women sew blue-coloured beads into the clothing of infants.

In the East, where the colour red has far greater significance than it does in the West, especially as a protector against evil, red beads are worn or carried by Indian children. In China and India the tiger is a protective symbol against

*Coral evidently in use in this fifteenth-century triptych of a madonna and child by David*

*A young boy standing in a turned and painted baby walker, holding a red coral rattle, by an unknown seventeenth-century English artist*

all bad spirits, and the Eye in particular. Indian babies may be given an amulet locket containing a package of tiger's meat. Tiger motifs are worn today, embroidered on to the caps and shoes of Chinese babies.

In European and American societies coral was used as a teething aid, but its real function was to act as a protective element in the battle against evil. Known since ancient times when it was prized as an aphrodisiac, coral was believed by the Greeks to have grown from the blood of the Gorgon Medusa.

31

*The Duchess of York and the Princess Elizabeth photographed in 1927, with the Princess clutching her coral necklace*

In time it came to be valued more for its amuletic powers, especially for first-born sons, than for its amatory associations.

From paintings and literature of the period, we know that coral was used in the creation of babies' rattles from the seventeenth century to the late nineteenth century. It seems likely that coral was in wide use before this time, as a fourteenth-century painting showing the Christ Child wearing a coral necklace would seem to suggest. A lack of sufficient documentation makes this difficult to prove. In any case, coral would have been an expensive material, and therefore it would have been available only to the minority who could afford it. Highly valued as a charm and often used to create rosaries, no doubt coral – and coral imitations – would have been peddled by unscrupulous dealers in such items.

Coral became permanently associated with childhood and in the sixteenth century, the term 'sucking his coral' would refer to an infant or toddler who was not yet deemed ready to begin the next phase of his, to us, shockingly early introduction to the adult world.

If we are to believe the newspapers of the eighteenth century, coral was sold as a teething aid and at this time it was known as 'gumstick'. But it is difficult for us to accept that such a precious substance, which was often fashioned into elaborate necklaces and bracelets, would have been given into the destructive grasp of an infant. Rattles surviving from the eighteenth and nineteenth centuries are quite ornate, usually made of silver, which was supposed to be protection against witches, but gold rattles are not unknown. Other than a coral 'gumstick', the rattle had clusters of silver bells attached and very often a whistle, or 'whissle', at it was advertised. Perhaps nurses used the rattles to entertain the infant, or perhaps infants were allowed to play with their coral rattles on Sundays and other important family days. Whatever the case, chased silver and coral rattles were popular christening presents, amongst those who could afford to give them, until the nineteenth century when germ theory undoubtedly contributed to coral's decline in popularity.

Surprisingly enough, old wives' tales and superstitions are still deeply embedded in our culture, and many people are unconscious of the fact. Although science is playing a large part in crushing our fears, replacing sense for nonsense, the combination of the extraordinary human reproductive system and the human mind will always create fears and therefore ways in which to deal with them.

## A LULLABY OF THE NATIVITY

Lullay, my liking, my dere son,
    my sweeting.
Lullay, my dere herte, my owen
    dere darling.

I saw a fair maiden
Sitten and sing:
She lulled a little child,
A swete lording.

That eche Lord is that
That made alle thing:
Of alle lordes he is Lord,
Of alle kinges King.

Ther was mekil melody
At that childes berth:
Alle tho wern in Hevene blis
They made mekil merth.

Aungele bright they song that
    night,
And seiden to that child:
'Blissed be thou, and so be she,
That is bothe mek and mild.'

Prey we now to that child,
And to his moder dere,
Graunt hem his blissing,
That now maken chere.

                        Anon

# Magic Stones

Stones have long been credited with possessing magical powers and certain stones have become associated with birth. Women who had conceived and wanted to be sure of producing a healthy child wore a stone, the lapis aquilaris, or eagle stone, which they bound with fabric around their left arm or thigh. The eagle stone, which was credited with sufficient powers to prevent haemorrhage, was used in cultures throughout the world, and it was known since earliest times. Many midwives carried the eagle stone which they gave women to hold during labour, and no doubt the stones were bought and sold along with other charms and trinkets. The eagle stone has been identified as limonite, or brown haematite, or haematite proper. Lodestone (magnetite) was supposed to hold the foetus in the body, while jasper was believed to help the foetus emerge. In China and India jade was worn as a birth amulet. Other semi-precious stones credited with special powers are agate, cornelian and onyx.

Just as astrologers believe that we are ruled by the positioning of the planets at the time of birth, and that the month in which we are born, represented by a zodiac sign, influences our behaviour, so some people think that the months of the year are influenced by a precious stone.

Over the years, the stones favoured for a particular month have changed somewhat. The old April stone, the bloodstone, has been replaced by the aquamarine. The pearl is now thought of as being the stone for the month of July and the ruby for August. The alexandrite is now thought of as the stone for September, and the sapphire for October.

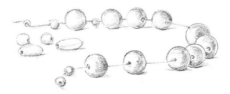

| Month | Zodiac sign | Precious stone | Symbol |
|---|---|---|---|
| January | Capricorn | Turquoise | Prosperity |
| February | Aquarius | Garnet | Fidelity |
| March | Pisces | Amethyst | Sincerity |
| April | Aries | Bloodstone | Courage |
| May | Taurus | Diamond | Innocence |
| June | Gemini | Emerald | Success in love |
| July | Cancer | Agate | Health and longevity |
| August | Leo | Cornelian | Satisfaction |
| September | Virgo | Sardonyx | Happiness in marriage |
| October | Libra | Chrysolite | Protection against madness |
| November | Scorpio | Opal | Hope |
| December | Sagittarius | Topaz | Fidelity |

It became fashionable to give infants gem stones of the saint corresponding to the month of the infant's birth.

| Month | Saint | Precious stone |
|---|---|---|
| January | St Peter | Jasper |
| February | St Andrew | Carbuncle |
| March | St James the Greater/St John | Emerald |
| April | St Philip | Cornelian |
| May | St Bartholomew | Chrysolite |
| June | St Thomas | Beryl |
| July | St Matthew | Topaz |
| August | St James the Less | Sardonyx |
| September | St Thaddeus | Chrysoprase |
| October | St Simon | Jacinth |
| November | St Matthias | Amethyst |
| December | St Paul | Sapphire |

# Foundlings

IT is sad, but true, that not all babies are wanted. This was far more obvious in the past when the attitudes of the day resulted in the death of thousands of infants who were placed outside the home to die, or to be taken and sold into slavery. Moses was one of the first foundlings known to our history. He was left to his fate in a basket on the banks of a river.

In many cases the infant would have been conceived outside marriage, or she would have been the daughter of a Roman family in urgent need of a son, or one of a pair of twins, or the last child in a family numbering fourteen already where there wasn't enough food to share, or a sickly, deformed infant who had little hope of survival at a time of primitive medical practice. So they were 'dropt', as it was known in the eighteenth century, in dark alleys and gutters, or out in the cold wet woods. Others were drowned in the river or put in bed between mother and father so that by morning they could no longer breathe. It has been estimated by historians of the eighteenth century that an infant was four times as likely to be a victim of homicide than anyone else.

In order to understand why people disposed of their babies in this way, we need to examine their motives. For thousands of years, until fairly recently in our history, women had little choice in the matter of how they lived their lives. As daughters they were quite often unwanted, especially in a household where it was hard for the parents to raise a dowry that would attract a suitor. With the exception of becoming a nun, marriage was seen as the only option in life. Once married, women would no longer belong to their fathers but to their husbands, symbolized by the 'giving away' of the bride in the Christian marriage ceremony.

If a young woman, of any class of society – although it was more likely to be those of the working classes as they had more day-by-day contact with men – found herself pregnant, her life would change. She became what is known to us from the nineteenth century as a 'fallen woman', the subject of numerous paintings when artists chose to depict these unfortunate women, thin, dishevelled and very often gravely ill, clutching their children to them as they huddled together under a damp railway bridge.

Despite the stories in the nineteenth century, being in domestic service was, in the seventeenth and eighteenth centuries, not a bad way of life, as Antonia Fraser points out in her book, *The Weaker Vessel*. Household servants were provided with food, clothing and shelter, and they were far better off than many others of their class who were faced with a daily struggle to provide themselves with just two of those three necessities. A girl, or woman, in service who found herself pregnant, as any woman might if she engaged in sexual activity without contraception, would most likely be cast into the street where, unable to provide for her infant, she would be forced to 'drop' it at the door of someone better off than herself: in a church porch, at the workhouse, or at an orphanage, or later, at a foundling hospital.

This was the case unless the wife of the household was unable to have children herself, when her husband might have a number of illegitimate children with his female servants. Many of our popular attitudes towards history today are formed by those ideas of the eighteenth and nineteenth centuries,when, in fact, it is important to remember that in the seventeenth century and earlier 'natural' children were looked upon with some benevolence. Many were well provided for and, if their father was a member of the aristocracy, they might even be accepted at court.

But it was during the eighteenth and nineteenth centuries that there appears to have been a greater incidence of infanticide than at any other time. The reasons are many and complex. First of all, the ways in which the populace was counted in the past were most inadequate by our standards. Despite an Act of Parliament, passed in 1538, which decreed that all births, baptisms, weddings and deaths should be recorded, numerous births went unrecorded. In order to record a birth, the mother had to give her name, which was something a woman without a father for the child preferred not to do. However, the church, ultimately responsible for burying people, even in a pauper's grave, would record the number of burials.

## THE LAMENTABLE BALLAD OF THE FOUNDLING OF SHOREDITCH

Come all ye Christian people,
  and listen to my tail
It is all about a doctor was
  travelling by the rail,
By the Heastern Counties
  Railway (vich the shares I
  don't desire,)
From Ixworth town in Suffolk,
  vich his name did not
  transpire.

A travelling from Bury this
  Doctor was employed
With a gentleman, a friend of
  his, vich his name was
  Captain Lloyd,
And on reaching Marks Tey
  Station, that is next beyond
  Colchester,
  a lady entered in to them
  most elegantly dressed.

She entered into the Carriage all
  with a tottering step,
And a pooty little Bayby upon
  her bussum slep;
The gentlemen received her with
  kindness and siwillaty,
Pitying this lady for her illness
  and debillaty . . .

A seein of her cryin, and shiverin
  and pail,
To her spoke this surging, the
  Ero of my tail;
Saysee 'You look unwell, ma'am:
  I'll elp you if I can,
And you may tell your case to
  me, for I'm a meddicle man.'

'Thank you, sir,' the lady said, 'I
  only look so pale,

Because I ain't accustom'd to
  travelling on the Rale;
I shall be better presnly, when
  I've ad some rest:'
And that pooty little Baby she
  squeeged it to her breast.

When at Shoreditch tumminus
  at length stopped the train,
This kind meddicle gentleman
  proposed his aid again.
'Thank you, sir,' the lady said,
  'for your kyindness dear;
My carridge and my osses is
  probibbly come here.

'Will you old this baby, please,
  vilst I step and see?'
The Doctor was a family man:
  'That I will,' says he.
Then the little child she kist, kist
  it very gently,
Vich was sucking his little fist,
  sleeping innocently.

With a sigh from her art, as
  though she would have bust it,
Then she gave the Doctor the
  child – wery kind he nust it:
Hup then the lady jumped hoff
  the bench she sat from,
Tumbled down the carridge
  steps
  and ran along the platform.

What could this pore Doctor do,
  bein' treated thus,
When the darling Baby woke,
  cryin' for its nuss?
Off he drove to a female friend,
  vich she was both kind and
  mild,

And igsplained to her the
  circumstance of this year little
  child.

That kind lady took the child
  instantly in her lap,
And made it very comfortable by
  giving it some pap;
And when she took its close off,
  what d'you think she found?
A couple of ten pun notes sewn
  up in its little gownd!

Also in its little close, was a note
  which did conwey,
That this little baby's parents
  lived in a handsome way
And for its Headucation they
  reglarly would pay,
And sirtingly like gentlefolks
  would claim the child one day,
If the Christian people who'd
  charge of it would say,
Per adwertisement in *The Times*,
  where the baby lay.

Lost in apoplexity, this pore
  meddicle man,
Like a sensable gentleman, to the
  Justice ran,
Which his name was Mr
  Hammill, a honorable beak,
That takes his seat in Worship
  Street four times a week.

'O Justice!' says the Doctor,
  'instrugt me what to do.
I've come up from the country,
  to throw myself on you;
My patients have no doctor to
  tend them in their ills

(There they are in Suffolk
  without their draffts and pills!).

'I've come up from the country,
  to know how I'll dispose
Of this pore little baby, and the
  twenty pun note, and the close,
And I want to go back to Suffolk,
  dear Justice, if you please,
And my patients wants their
  Doctor, and their Doctor
  wants his feez.'

Up spoke Mr Hammill, sittin' at
  his desk,
'This year application does me
  much perplesk;
What I do adwise you, is to leave
  this babby
In the Parish where it was left by
  its mother shabby.'

The Doctor from his Worship
  sadly did depart –
He might have left the baby, but
  he hadn't got the heart
To go for to leave that Hinnocent,
  has the laws allows,
To the tender mussies of the
  Union House.

Mother, who left this little one
  on a stranger's knee,
Think how cruel you have been,
  and how good was he!
Think, if you've been guilty,
  innocent was she;
And do not take unkindly this
  little word of me:
Heaven be merciful to us all,
  sinners as we be!

W. M. Thackeray

*Almost an everyday event, one would think, to see the faces of the men as a foundling is placed in front of them in George Bernard O'Neil's (1828–1917) painting,* The Foundling, *of 1862*

In the workhouse, it is quite possible that the overseer would not record the birth of a child who seemed unlikely to survive, only concerning himself with recording deaths. Therefore, while we have an idea of the number of deaths, we cannot know the number of births, but what strikes us most is that the number of deaths seems appallingly high.

Another thing to consider is that until the nineteenth century, people were not as sentimental as they are today. The hardships of life were greater, people did not live to the age they do now and death was accepted as far more commonplace. That is not to say that mothers had no feelings for their children; on the contrary, but the birth of an illegitimate child was a threat to a woman's survival.

Fortunately, the plight of unwanted infants has always concerned some people. Traditionally, monasteries and convents usually accepted the children left on their doorsteps and societies seemed to have made some provision for orphans, children whose parents had died or abandoned their offspring. Ancient Greeks and Romans had a legalized system of adoption whereby the adopted child received full legal rights. But adoption soon became a synonym for slavery and the practice fell into disrepute.

One of the first foundling hospitals to be recorded was established by Datheus, Archbishop of Milan in AD 787. His intentions were to help parents avoid eternal damnation in killing their children, by bringing them instead to a hospice. Here the children were baptized and entrusted to nurses until they reached the age of seven when a suitable apprenticeship was found for them.

Charitable institutions can be supported only by a good economy, by the generosity of a ruling family, by the state, or by private donations. In times of economic stress, orphanages, along with other organizations, have to struggle to maintain themselves. A number were maintained in Europe throughout the Middle Ages, and the cities of Venice, Lisbon, Amsterdam and Paris accepted the orphaned offspring of sailors and soldiers, but some hospitals became dumping grounds for unwanted children rather than homes for legitimate orphans. In most cases, children were placed in homes as wards of the state, their inheritances, if any, denied them. Little is known of these practices or the institutions that fulfilled the role of orphanages, but they have always existed in a society which has sufficient finances to be able to support them. In the absence of an orphanage, hospice or home, unwanted children were left to die.

In England, the parish workhouse was a part of society from the fifteenth century. Children who were 'dropt', left abandoned on the street and in doorways, were usually taken to the local workhouse, where, as a result of inadequate care, most of them died. In 1767, an Act was passed, which stipulated that all infants in parish workhouses must be farmed out to wet nurses who lived outside the workhouse. These wet nurses were paid 2s. 6d a week per child, with a bonus if the child lived for a year.

In the eighteenth century one individual was concerned by the infants he

*A popular subject for painters: the agony of a mother depositing her young child at the Foundling Hospital, painted in 1850 by Henry Nelson O'Neil (1817–80)*

saw abandoned in the city of London. By some accounts, especially if we are to believe the engravings of the period, infants were now being left on dung heaps and at street corners. Thomas Coram, a shipwright who had worked in both England and America before he retired in Rotherhithe in 1719, managed to persuade twenty-two noble ladies to sign a petition stating that they would contribute towards the establishment and running of a 'foundling' hospital. The Duke of Bedford agreed to be governor. The hospital opened its doors in 1741 in premises in Hatton Garden. Its charter proclaimed it as 'The Hospital for the Maintenance and Education of Exposed and Deserted Young Children', and it was supported by six dukes, eleven earls and many other peers, city businessmen and even artists. William Hogarth was one such artist

*A sixteenth-century painting entitled* The Nurture and Marriage of the Foundlings *from a church in Siena, Italy. Organizations existed in Italy since Roman times for the care and upbringing of orphans*

who supported the hospital by making donations of his work for sale. Indeed, Hogarth and his wife raised several foundlings from the hospital at their home in Chiswick during the 1760s.

In the early days of the hospital, the number of children brought to the hospital doors far exceeded those who were accepted. The hospital took in only those children who looked reasonably healthy, but nonetheless dying children were brought to the hospital by parents who hoped to avoid paying for a burial. In the initial charter the hospital porters were instructed not to let people leave their offspring before the infant had been formally admitted. 'No Child shall be returned who is not above the Age of Two Months, or who has not the French Pox, Evil, Leprosy or Disease of the like Nature.' The child was inspected by the nurses and hospital apothecary, and then described and numbered on a piece of paper which was taped to its clothing. The next day the child would be presented to the Daily Committee, re-described in some instances, and named. The following Sunday the child would be baptized.

The governing board named the children, which meant that many of these unwanted infants grew up with the names of some of England's oldest and most prestigious families such as Marlborough, Norfolk, Montague and Richmond. Infants were also named after famous people – William Shakespeare, for example, Oliver Cromwell, or Anthony Vandyke – and names were taken from popular novels of the day.

The actual day-by-day care of these infants troubled the board of philanthropic governors, who had few ideas on the subject. They asked the College of Physicians for help, an act which spawned a number of books and essays on child-raising. In 1748 a pamphlet was published by the General Committee of the hospital entitled *An Essay upon Nursing, and the Management of Children from Their Birth to Three Years of Age*. The basis of this pamphlet was, in fact, a letter written to one of the governors by Dr William Cadogan (1711–97), MA, MD Oxon., FRS, FRCP, who denounced contemporary child-rearing practices. He wrote that 'the general Practice is, as soon as a Child is born, to cram a Dab of Butter and Sugar down its Throat, a little Oil, Panada, Caudal, or some such unwholesome Mess.' Cadogan rejected this, believing that nature took care of things, since, as mother's milk very often did not come until three days after the child was born, the child could not be hungry until that time.

Dr Cadogan, who became very well known and was later appointed

*Mrs Emma Brownlow King specialized in painting domestic scenes with children. Here she depicts a christening of foundlings at the Thomas Coram Foundling Hospital*

Honorary Physician to the hospital, advocated frequent changes of clothing for infants, rather than keeping them wrapped in the same clothes for days at a time, as was common at the time. People believed that a child would catch cold if its head was exposed, and that to unwrap its swaddling bands too often could cause illness as babies would be robbed of their essential juices. Cadogan took a stand also on swaddling, and although he was not the only doctor at the time who believed that it was bad for babies to have their limbs confined, it is Cadogan who is credited today with the decline in the practice of swaddling which took place during the late eighteenth century. Cadogan's other contribution to infant welfare was to recommend that infants be breast-fed whenever possible.

For a while after the hospital opened, it was the fashionable thing amongst the wealthy to contribute funds. However, some moralists disagreed with the

*Lady Bracknell*: Are your parents living?

*Jack*: I have lost both my parents.

*Lady Bracknell*: To lose one parent, Mr Worthing, may be regarded as a misfortune; to lose both looks like carelessness. Who was your father? He was evidently a man of some wealth. Was he born in what the Radical papers call the purple of commerce, or did he rise from the ranks of the aristocracy?

*Jack*: I am afraid I really don't know. The fact is, Lady Bracknell, I said I had lost my parents. It would be nearer the truth to say that my parents seem to have lost me . . . I don't actually know who I am by birth. I was . . . well, I was found.

*Lady Bracknell*: Found!

*Jack*: The late Mr Thomas Cardew, an old gentleman of a very charitable and kindly disposition, found me, and gave me the name of Worthing, because he happened to have a first-class ticket for Worthing in his pocket at the time. Worthing is a place in Sussex. It is a seaside resort.

*Lady Bracknell*: Where did the charitable gentleman who had a first-class ticket for this seaside resort find you?

*Jack*: [*Gravely.*] In a hand-bag.

*Lady Bracknell*: A hand-bag?

*Jack*: [*Very seriously.*] Yes, Lady Bracknell. I was in a hand-bag – a somewhat large, black leather hand-bag, with handles to it – an ordinary hand-bag in fact.

*Lady Bracknell*: In what locality did this Mr James, or Thomas, Cardew come across this ordinary hand-bag?

*Jack*: In the cloakroom at Victoria Station. It was given to him in mistake for his own.

*Lady Bracknell*: The cloakroom at Victoria Station?

*Jack*: Yes. The Brighton line.

*Lady Bracknell*: The line is immaterial. Mr Worthing, I confess I feel somewhat bewildered by what you have just told me. To be born, or at any rate bred, in a hand-bag, whether it had handles or not, seems to me to display a contempt for the ordinary decencies of family life that reminds one of the worst excesses of the French Revolution. And I presume you know what that unfortunate movement led to? As for the particular locality in which the hand-bag was found, a cloakroom at a railway station might serve to conceal a social indiscretion – has probably, indeed, been used for that purpose before now – but it could hardly be regarded as an assured basis for a recognized position in good society.

*Jack*: May I ask you then what you would advise me to do? I need hardly say I would do anything in the world to ensure Gwendolen's happiness.

*Lady Bracknell*: I would strongly advise you, Mr Worthing, to try and acquire some relations as soon as possible, and to make a definite effort to produce at any rate one parent, of either sex, before the season is quite over.

*The Importance of Being Earnest,*
Oscar Wilde

whole concept of the hospital, believing that it encouraged prostitution by relieving women of their unwanted offspring. Although considerable sums of money were coming in, the governors found that it was insufficient to pay the wages of all the nursing help and servants needed to watch over the infants who had been admitted in the four or five years since the hospital opened its doors. The hospital had started with two wet nurses and four dry nurses with other nurses available on demand, plus a number of servants, but this proved an inadequate number to provide sufficient care of the infants. Larger premises had to be found, not only for the growing number of admissions, but for the older children who needed to be taught skills before apprenticeships could be secured for them. The hospital spread its wings to the provinces where children were sent to be cared for by nurses employed by the hospital.

The subsequent application for funds by the governors to Parliament in 1756 was successful, and the foundling hospital set about establishing new rules. The hospital became known as the Foundling Hospital of England and children were sent from all over the country. The acceptance age was increased to six months, and sickly infants were transferred to a medical hospital. Overseers in the parish workhouses brought their unwanted infants to the hospital and babies were delivered from all over the country, often by vagrants who would charge a price per head. Many infants did not survive the journey. This indiscriminate admission did not help the hospital at all as the new funds were quickly used up. In the 1760s changes were made to the manner in which children were admitted. Each application was investigated and as a result the infants taken in were, generally, genuine orphans, usually those of soldiers and sailors, infants who had been turned away by a parish overseer, or offspring of married women whose husbands had deserted them and who had no means of support. By the early 1800s the hospital received only illegitimate infants whose mothers were otherwise of 'previous good character', and whose fathers had deserted them, and this practice continued well into the nineteenth century when the necessity for the hospital decreased.

Foundling hospitals were the subjects of numerous Victorian paintings, many of which depicted mothers leaving their babies in baskets at the hospital's doors. We must assume, therefore, given the moralistic tendency in art of the period, that foundling hospitals fulfilled an essential role in society. The reason that there are few orphanages, for that is what foundling hospitals finally became, today is because of several factors.

The devastation of two world wars resulted in the baby boom years of the 1950s when women were encouraged to stay at home and raise their families. Children were wanted – more perhaps than ever before. For the first time women had the means to decide on the number of children they wished to give birth to through contraception, thus lessening the incidence of unwanted pregnancies and unwanted children. Of course, we are not in an ideal world and some children are still unwanted, but these days in many cases they are fostered to caring families, or made the responsibility of the social services, a government-sponsored agency, or placed in an orphanage. A 'foundling', such as we would think of during the nineteenth century, would be today a newsworthy item likely to attract the attention of the national press.

Families today are much smaller, and in some instances this is not by choice. Women are having babies later in life than at any other time in our history which means that their chances of becoming pregnant are considerably reduced. Fertility clinics have opened in relatively recent years to help childless women who desire children. Today a woman who is unable to bear a child herself, or whose partner cannot have children, looks to adoption, artificial insemination, in vitro fertilization or surrogate parenting.

Adoption, whereby the child would retain his or her inheritance and be entitled to full legal rights, was first legalized in the United States in 1851 in the state of Massachusetts. Other states followed slowly, some taking almost one hundred years. England did not bring its laws on adoption into similar order until 1926. Artificial insemination is no longer the hotly debated issue that it was. Surrogate parenting is an issue which is now the subject of many legal cases, the outcome of which will not become immediately obvious for a number of years, perhaps even until those children born to surrogate mothers are old enough to speak for themselves. Today, in an age of 'nuclear' families, we are concerned with the need to produce more children, an idea which would have been inconceivable less than two hundred years ago.

# IN THE STRAW

The clamouring of the chapel bells woke the whole castle. Everyone, from the smallest stable boy to the visiting drunken lord who had over-indulged in his host's ale and was now stretched out with the dogs under the table in the great hall, rolled over in their sleep and sat up dazed.

Soldiers reached for their swords, women clutched their bedmates, children cried, dogs started barking, and kitchen boys concealed themselves in the few nooks and crannies that the castle offered. The bells did not cease. The Countess was big with child. Her time must have come.

The steward was the first one to arrive in the kitchen. He hauled two scruffy boys from the corner where they were hiding by the embers of the big fire and dispatched them to the chapel. The bells might have to be rung all night, and whoever was pulling the ropes now would need to be relieved. No one would get any more sleep that night, except, perhaps, the drunken lord who, having satisfied himself that he was not in any immediate danger, was now snoring so loudly that some of the dogs had moved and settled themselves elsewhere.

The cook stumbled over the threshold, sleepy-eyed, followed by his assistants. Under his directions the great fire was stoked and refuelled. Complaining about the cold and the dark night, several kitchen boys were sent to fetch more wood. Two of the strongest men lifted an enormous cauldron on to an iron stand over the heat. No one had seen the baker. The butler appeared, keys in hand, looking for his dispensers who would help him bring up wine and ale from the cellar. If her ladyship gave birth to a son, they would be feasting for days; if she had a girl, the feast would only last one day; and if the child, or its mother, died, then there would be a mourning. In any event, food would be required. All the steward hoped was that the baby would be born before too much food had been prepared. Waste was something his lordship despised.

Leaving the kitchens in the command of the cook, the steward set off across the keep for the stables. No wonder the kitchen boys didn't want to set foot outside. It was still dark, the night was bitterly cold and he had trouble finding his way but the sounds from the stables acted as his guide. It was much warmer inside the stables, but still he could see the breath of men and horses hanging in the chill air. It appeared that the stables had been awake for some time. The horses, unused to sudden activity in peace time, were restless and making a great deal of noise. Grooms were at work tacking up

and stable boys got under everyone's feet, more hindrance than help.

Messengers would need to be dispatched to members of the lord's family who lived in castles and manors all over the country. These men, who would be gone for weeks, would need horses, clothing, food and money for their journeys. The king at his court in London would need to be told of the birth of one of his cousins. One messenger would have to cross water and travel as far as Calais. The steward did not envy that man. There was no telling when the castle would see his return. Perhaps the captain would have enough sense this time to send an unmarried man who had no wife to make a nuisance of herself while her husband was away. The men in the stables were hard at work. No one knew if it would be tonight or tomorrow morning before the messengers could leave. It all depended on the saints, for whom the bells were being rung.

The steward did not look in on the chapel. He walked briskly, stumbling a little in his hurry to get back behind the castle walls. He reached the retainers' hall where the soldiers were housed. Those who weren't on sentry duty stood around in groups, half-dressed, idle and useless as soldiers often are without a war to occupy them. The steward spoke to the captain. The stables needed extra help, so did the boys ringing bells in the chapel. Shouting commands, the captain brought the garrison to order.

The steward crossed the hall, heading for the solar where his lord waited, impatiently pacing up and down in front of a huge fire. The room was bright with candles and firelight, in contrast to the darkened bed chamber which the steward could see leading from the solar. This was the lord's third child but he was young and not yet used to breeding children. In future years, he would absent himself and go hunting, sending messengers back to the castle to find out how his wife was faring. The lady was younger than her husband and braver, too, as far as the steward could gather from castle gossip. He could make her out in her great bed which had been hung with drapes.

'Can't you do something?' the lord was asking the chaplain. The fat old priest wrung his hands. He avoided the lord as much as possible, wary of the man's impatience with heavenly matters.

'It's in God's hands,' the priest murmured. 'I myself have no great powers. I am only His servant, willing to carry out His every wish.'

The lord stopped pacing and turned to the priest, his back to the fire.

'Well, you may be God's servant but you're also mine, so get back to the chapel and start praying.'

Speechless with shock, the priest gathered his robes about himself and scuttled towards the door. He had spoken to the Archbishop about his employer's irreverent attitude and the Archbishop had promised to have a word with the king. Obviously, nothing had been said so far.

The steward stepped aside to let the priest pass. He should feel sorry for the him, the butt of the castle's jokes, but somehow he couldn't find it in himself to do so. Once, in need of consolation shortly after his first wife had died, he went to see the priest. As steward, there were few people to whom he could turn and he believed the priest to be one of them, but the old man had sent a servant to say he was too busy to see the steward.

'Well, steward,' said the lord, 'is everything ready?'

'It is, my lord.'

'If only the saints would ease my poor wife's burden.' The lord shook his head.

'Shall I have more ale fetched?' the steward asked, thinking that strong ale

50

would help more than any saint at the moment.

'Maybe, maybe . . .' the lord was lost in thought, staring into the fire.

He is praying for a son, thought the steward, as he approached the lady's bed chamber. So would I, in his shoes, with only two daughters to survive me.

One of the women of the bed chamber saw him approach and blocked his entry to the room, though he had no intention of setting foot over the threshold. Birthing babies was women's business. His wife used to tell him that a man in the birthing room was bad luck.

'Shall I have more ale fetched, mistress?' he asked at the door.

'If the baby doesn't come soon she won't have need of it,' replied the woman grimly.

The steward couldn't help peering over her head. He saw the midwife's back, as she bent over her patient. The old crone had been staying in the castle for a week now. Drunk as often as not, and chasing the kitchen boys so that they dreaded to take her food, a necessity as the lord wouldn't have her at his table, the old woman was nonetheless supposed to be skilled at her work.

In her great bed the lady of the castle was restless. She didn't mind the midwife and was willing to submit to her commands, but she would have liked just a few more candles in the room. The light from the fire alone created flickering shadows on the wall. At least it was warm. The midwife had insisted that the drapes be taken down from the main hall and hung up in her room for the duration of the birth. Her husband had been furious and he suspected that the old woman's demands were not for his wife's benefit, but to irritate him because he had never allowed her to dine with him in the main hall.

The midwife required the other women to keep their distance – which wasn't too difficult as the old woman always smelled of sour wine – and

occupy themselves with setting out the baby's swaddling bands, his cloaks and bed covers. Being February, there were no flowers to be found, but they had a jar of honey and some salt tied up in a sack with which to rub the baby. Straw had been strewn all over the floor and a great pile of it was stacked up on a pallet next to the bed.

A sturdy wooden rocking cradle sat empty in a corner, its deep hood keeping out the wind which squeezed through the castle walls. The cradle was only recently vacated by a sister who was now, awoken by the unusual nocturnal commotion, staggering about on leather leading reins in an adjoining chamber, being watched over by one of the girls from the kitchen. The wet nurse, who might or might not be needed, sat patiently by the fire, watching, thinking of her own child only recently lost.

The midwife told the other women to help their ladyship on to the straw pallet on the floor. There was no point in ruining good bed linens. She'd delivered enough babies to know when one wanted to enter the world and it seemed that high-ranking babies were no different. She'd enjoyed her stay in the castle, and if this birth was successful she would be asked back. But first of all she had to make a safe delivery.

It took a while for the kitchen to realize, over the clatter of the pans, that the bells had stopped ringing. The cook stopped what he was doing and wiped his hands on his apron. He felt sure it would be another girl, but the butler wasn't convinced.

A boy came scurrying into the large room carrying an empty jug of ale. A grin was stretched across a face that was otherwise pinched with cold.

The cook advanced upon him, sensing that the boy knew something. The entire kitchen turned its attention to the scrawny boy who almost lost his ability to speak under the gaze of so many eyes.

'Well,' said the cook. 'What is it? Boy or girl? Alive or dead?'

'It's a boy,' the child squeaked, holding his arms out wide. 'A great big boy. I saw him myself.'

'No, you did not,' corrected the butler. 'They wouldn't let you into her ladyship's chamber.'

'I saw him, I did,' the boy persisted. 'His lordship showed him to me.'

The kitchen laughed. The lord showing his baby to this scrap of a kitchen boy.

'Babies aren't that big,' said the baker and he imitated the boy by holding his arms out wide.

'This one is,' said the boy, 'and it's covered in gold.'

The baker snorted. The things those boys dream up. He turned his back on the youngster and went about preparing more food. Taking their cue from the baker, the rest of the kitchen ignored the boy.

But the boy spoke the truth. He'd been in the lord's solar collecting the empty jug of ale when one of her ladyship's women walked in carrying the baby. It was a big bundle, wrapped in clothes studded with gold and silver and a thick cloak of white fur. The boy had never seen anything like it. The lord reached for his son and held him awkwardly.

'Look,' he said, to the room in general. 'My son.' He held the baby out. They stood in a group: the steward, the fat old priest who had been hauled off his knees in church and dragged to the solar in case the baby needed baptizing immediately and the kitchen boy who was clutching the jug, eyes wide. Neither priest nor steward had much interest in babies, but they smiled and nodded politely. But the kitchen boy was transfixed. A golden baby, wrapped in furs. The biggest baby he'd ever seen.

Back in her own bed, sitting up against the pillows, her ladyship smiled at the scene outside her door. She was very pleased with herself. A boy, at last. If she could produce one boy, there could be others. No doubt her husband would buy her those precious jewels she wanted now. She reached under one of the pillows and discreetly pulled out a small muslin sack which was filled with herbs and tiny stones. The midwife had given it to her, and told her to clutch it tightly and pray to St Agnes. She kissed the little sack. There was much to plan. A big christening, bigger than anyone had seen in a long time, with six attendants for the baby, a journey to court; perhaps the king might be persuaded to see his young male cousin – he'd never shown much interest in her daughters before, but now things were going to be very different.

INFANT SORROW

My mother groan'd! my father
    wept,
Into the dangerous world I leapt:
Helpless, naked, piping loud:
Like a fiend hid in a cloud.

Struggling in my father's hands,
Striving against my swadling
    bands,
Bound and weary I thought best
To sulk upon my mother's
    breast.

             William Blake

# BIRTHING

# Waiting for the Stork

Gloomy night embrac'd the
    place
Where the noble Infant lay.
The Babe look't up and shew'd
    his face;
In spite of darkness, it was day.
It was thy day, Sweet! and did
    rise
Not from the East, but from
    thine eyes.

*Hymn of the Nativity*
Richard Crashaw

UNTIL this century women gave birth unaided, except by other women. This was strongly connected to the idea that childbirth was unclean and therefore best left to the midwife who was a social outcast anyway. The image of the midwife in history was crystallized in the drunken Sairey Gamp in Dickens's story of *Martin Chuzzlewit*. Midwives have since been thought of as Mrs Gamps, elderly slatterns, no longer able to have children themselves, who not only delivered babies but performed abortions, told fortunes and took in washing to supplement their incomes.

Early cultures in Egypt and the Middle East treated midwives well, but after the fall of the Roman Empire, midwives have been viewed, generally, as being on the lowest rung of the social ladder. By the fourteenth century their social status was such that they were usually isolated by communities. In primitive tribes, midwives were expected to live alone, tainted with the 'unclean' nature that is associated with childbirth in those cultures.

During the Middle Ages midwives were suspected of everything. In towns and villages ignorance and fear created numerous superstitions amongst the populace, and fingers pointed at the local midwife when anything inexplicable or out of the ordinary occurred. Most often, midwives were suspected of being witches, or, at the very least, of meddling in witchcraft, and many midwives died, blamed for the mysterious death of someone they had never met. As childbirth was viewed with such enormous fear, anything connected to it was automatically suspect. Witches were believed to use the nails and hair of a newborn baby, as well as the placenta from the mother in their craft, and midwives were credited with all kinds of supernatural powers.

Midwives were blamed if a birth went badly and seldom praised if it went well unless they were fortunate enough to be hired by a grateful *and* wealthy parent, in which case the rewards were substantial. However, successful midwives who attended royal births were well rewarded if they managed to deliver a healthy child. Madame Péronne, midwife to Henrietta Maria, was given £1,000 by Charles I when she delivered the boy who would grow up to become Charles II.

The church attempted to maintain control of midwives and, in some cases, it led witch-hunts amongst midwives in communities. Local church figures expected a midwife to elicit from the unwed woman in labour the name of the father of the child so that he might be traced and maintenance could be enforced. In the seventeenth century, in England, the church required midwives to apply for licences to operate; but while records exist to prove that a number of midwives did indeed receive licences, it is impossible to even guess at the numbers of midwives working at this time, licensed or unlicensed. Many midwives carried out their work in remote villages, far away from the jurisdiction of the church.

There was, surprisingly, comparatively little concern about midwifery, childbirth practices and doctors in the past. Much prejudice existed, first against the inept midwife and later the untrained medical practitioner, but it was not until the late nineteenth and early twentieth centuries that extensive reports were published on infant mortality figures and childbirth practices.

*Cleopatra giving birth in the position still favoured by many women. Taken from a relief on the temple of Esneth*

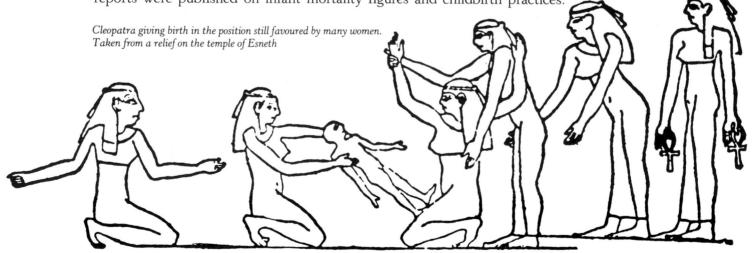

*The young Duke of York dressed in elaborate clothes for this* Portrait of King Charles I and Queen Henrietta Maria, the Prince of Wales and the Duke of York seated on the Terrace with a View of the Palace Westminster Beyond, *by Sir Anthony Van Dyck (1599–1641)*

Concern amongst the medical profession at this time was related to raising the standards of obstetrics and the education of both midwives and doctors. In England, for example, the Midwives Act of 1902 meant that only properly certified, state-registered midwives could be present at a birth. Uncertified women were given until 1910 to obtain state registration. In America, the state of New York led the field in midwife training and certification, and established the first school for midwives in 1911. Each state had its own laws. Massachusetts outlawed midwives altogether between 1900 and 1930, while other states had no legislation governing midwives.

Alongside the history of the changes in the role of midwifery coexists the rise of the role of the man-midwife, and, later, the obstetrician. During the Middle Ages it was forbidden to dissect corpses, therefore the midwife would be required to call in the local butcher, barber or sow gelder, to help her deliver a dead child so that both mother and child could be given a proper burial. These men became known as men-midwives and they were called upon if the woman in labour was experiencing any difficulties that the midwife felt incapable of handling.

The midwife in medieval Europe was seen as preferable to these male midwives, who arrived with tools which invariably resulted in the death of the unborn child and, not infrequently, the maiming of the mother. The man-midwife was not called in until the last moment and by this time there was almost nothing anyone could do to help, especially someone who had little knowledge of female anatomy and childbirth practices. In any event, most women would not allow a man to attend them and any man admitted to the birthing chamber would be obliged, for the sake of modesty, to assist with the birth with his head sticking out of the top of a sheet, without actually looking at what he was supposed to be doing. Some men even wore women's clothes to conceal their identities.

A small number of manuals on midwifery were produced in the fifteenth and sixteenth centuries. They owed their origins to Ancient Greek and Latin texts. For two thousand years the ideas of Aristotle were the basis for all works on obstetrics. He believed that women provided the right kind of environment for the foetus but it was the man who determined its soul and spirituality. This gave credence to the idea of woman as a vessel, a kind of nursery pot in which seedlings could grow, and contributed to the passive role that women played in the past.

With a few exceptions the manuals were written by men, amongst them a man who began his career as a Dominican monk. They dealt with many aspects of childbirth, including abnormal presentations that posed problems for the midwife; they argued over appropriate positions in which women should give birth and the role of the midwife. Very often the manuals were written in Latin, which meant that they would have been accessible only to a limited audience, and probably a male audience at that.

Jane Sharp was one midwife who wrote a book entitled *The Midwives' Book or The Whole Art of Midwifery*, which was published in 1671. But it was the

59

nineteenth century before women were writing in any great numbers, giving advice to each other. Male doctors, such as Dr William Buchan, author of *Advice to Mothers*, 1803, and Thomas Bull, who wrote *Hints to Mothers during the Period of Pregnancy and in the Lying-In Room*, 1864, tackled the subject of the mother's clothing. During pregnancy, Dr Buchan forbade women to wear tight necklaces, tight garters, 'or any ligatures which may refrain the easy motions of the limbs' or obstruct the circulation of the blood. Most doctors deplored the wearing of stays, and suggested that tight-lacing caused miscarriages. If a corset must be worn, they recommended that it be the 'gestation' type, which had wide hip gores and expanded also at the front.

On the whole, doctors advised women to wear wrappers and capes and loose maternity dresses that they had specially made for their pregnancies. Examples of these clothes have not survived in any great number, and those that exist date from the late nineteenth century. It seems that the majority of women let out their ordinary dresses to accommodate their larger shapes. The specially made maternity dresses of the nineteenth century were made without a waist seam in the Princess style, popular from around the mid-century, when it was fitted over crinolines and bustles. The top section opened so that a nursing mother could breast-feed her child without having to disrobe completely.

Later in the century, female followers of the Aesthetic Movement adopted loose, flowing, medieval-style robes, which must have been far easier to wear. Many of these women not only loosened their corsets underneath these dresses but also discarded them altogether. By the 1920s maternity gowns, sold by London stores such as Dickins & Jones, were illustrated in catalogues and magazines alongside tea and rest gowns, invalid gowns and matinée jackets. The models were always pencil-thin, showing no signs of pregnancy at all. Maternity gowns, made of crêpe-de-Chine or chiffon velvet, were nonetheless loose-fitting. In the 1940s, the American designer Adrian made one of the first fashion-conscious two-piece maternity outfits.

Before doctors' advice was readily available, the woman in labour took her cue from the midwife. Arriving at a lying-in chamber, the midwife would insist that all doors be unlocked and any recently sewn garments be unpicked, in order to give the mother every opportunity for a speedy delivery, symbolically anyway. She might give the labouring woman a special kind of belt, or girdle, to wear around her abdomen which was supposed to induce

*American Indian women tied scarves around their abdomens and suspended themselves from ropes to induce delivery*

the child to emerge, and an eagle stone to clutch in her hand. The midwife might rub the vaginal area with butter or oil, which were thought to ease delivery, or put a magnet between the woman's legs which was believed to help draw out the child. Some midwives administered wine or broth, and in some instances, hard liquor, to the mother.

The attendant women would lay out the linens, prepare the swaddling bands and help by keeping food and drink warm. These women were known as 'gossips', and they became sponsors of the child and would take some responsibility in providing for it in the event that the mother died. In this way, they assumed an unofficial role which was similar to both a godparent and guardian. Gossips liked to make sure that the mother wore some garment of her husband's during labour in the hope that some of the pain would pass to him. Gossips attended births until the eighteenth century, when the practice started to die out. No doubt this had something to do with the presence of the man-midwife and his desire to be alone with the labouring woman so that others would not witness the tools he used to deliver the child.

Herbs were used extensively but certain kinds were never taken until labour began, such as juniper, poke root, rue, tansy and wormwood. (Interestingly enough, the World Health Organization estimates that 85 per cent of the world's population still use herbs as a major source of treatment for all kinds of problems.)

61

Mr Pecksniff had been to the undertaker, and was now upon his way to another officer in the train of mourning: a female functionary, a nurse, and watcher, and performer of nameless offices about the persons of the dead: whom he had recommended. Her name, as Mr Pecksniff gathered from a scrap of writing in his hand, was Gamp; her residence in Kingsgate Street, High Holborn. So Mr Pecksniff, in a hackney cab, was rattling over Holborn stones, in quest of Mrs Gamp.

This lady lodged at a bird-fancier's, next door but one to the celebrated mutton-pie shop, and directly opposite to the original cat's-meat warehouse; the renown of which establishments was duly heralded on their respective fronts. It was a little house, and this was the more convenient; for Mrs Gamp being, in her highest walk of art, a monthly nurse, or, as her signboard boldly had it, 'Midwife,' and lodging in the first-floor front, was easily assailable at night by pebbles, walking-sticks, and fragments of tobacco-pipe: all much more efficacious than the street-door knocker, which was so constructed as to wake the street with ease, and even spread alarms of fire in Holborn, without making the smallest impression on the premises to which it was addressed.

It chanced on this particular occasion, that Mrs Gamp had been up all the previous night, in attendance upon a ceremony to which the usage of gossips has given that name which expresses, in two syllables, the curse pronounced on Adam. It chanced that Mrs Gamp had not been regularly engaged, but had been called in at a crisis, in consequence of her great repute, to assist another professional lady with her advice; and thus it happened that, all points of interest in the case being over, Mrs Gamp had come home again to the bird-fancier's, and gone to bed. So when Mr Pecksniff drove up in the hackney cab, Mrs Gamp's curtains were drawn close, and Mrs Gamp was fast asleep behind them . . .

Mr Pecksniff tried the latch, and shook it, causing a cracked bell inside to ring most mournfully; but no one came . . .

Mr Pecksniff, in the innocence of his heart, applied himself to the knocker; but at the first double knock every window in the street became alive with female heads; and before he could repeat the performance whole troops of married ladies (some about to trouble Mrs Gamp themselves very shortly) came flocking round the steps, all crying out with one accord, and with uncommon interest, 'Knock at the winder, sir, knock at the winder. Lord bless you, don't lose no more time than you can help; knock at the winder!'

Acting upon this suggestion, and borrowing the driver's whip for the purpose, Mr Pecksniff soon made a commotion among the first-floor flower-pots, and roused Mrs Gamp, whose voice – to the great satisfaction of the matrons – was heard to say, 'I'm coming.'

'He's as pale as a muffin,' said one lady, in allusion to Mr Pecksniff.

'So he ought to be, if he's the feelings of a man,' observed another.

A third lady (with her arms folded) said she wished he had chosen any other time for fetching Mrs Gamp, but it always happened so with *her*.

It gave Mr Pecksniff much uneasiness to find, from these remarks, that he was supposed to have come to Mrs Gamp upon an errand touching – not the close of life, but the other end. Mrs Gamp herself was under the same impression, for, throwing open the window, she cried behind the curtains, as she hastily attired herself:

'Is it Mrs Perkins?'

'No!' returned Mr Pecksniff, sharply. 'Nothing of the sort.'

'What, Mr Whilks!' cried Mrs Gamp. 'Don't say it's you, Mr Whilks, and that poor creetur Mrs Whilks with not even a pincushion ready. Don't say it's you, Mr Whilks!'

'It isn't Mr Whilks,' said Pecksniff. 'I don't know the man. Nothing of the kind. A gentleman is dead; and some person being wanted in the house, you have been recommended by Mr Mould the undertaker.'

As she was by this time in a condition to appear, Mrs Gamp, who had a face for all occasions, looked out of the window with her mourning countenance, and said she would be down directly. But the matrons took it very ill that Mr Pecksniff's mission was of so unimportant a kind; and the lady with her arms folded rated him in good round terms, signifying that she would be glad to know what he meant by terrifying delicate females 'with his corpses'; and giving it as her opinion that he was quite ugly enough to know better. The other ladies were not at all behind-hand in expressing similar sentiments; and the children, of whom some scores had now collected, hooted and defied Mr Pecksniff quite savagely. So when Mrs Gamp appeared, the unoffending gentleman was glad to hustle her with very little ceremony into the cabriolet, and drive off, overwhelmed with popular execration . . .

She was a fat old woman, this Mrs Gamp, with a husky voice and a moist eye, which she had a remarkable power of turning up, and only showing the white of it. Having very little neck, it cost

her some trouble to look over herself, if one may say so, at those to whom she talked. She wore a very rusty black gown, rather the worse for snuff, and a shawl and bonnet to correspond. In these dilapidated articles of dress she had, on principle, arrayed herself, time out of mind, on such occasions as the present; for this at once expressed a decent amount of veneration for the deceased, and invited the next of kin to present her with a fresher suit of weeds: an appeal so frequently successful, that the very fetch and ghost of Mrs Gamp, bonnet and all, might be seen hanging up, any hour in the day, in at least a dozen of the second-hand clothes shops about Holborn. The face of Mrs Gamp – the nose in particular – was somewhat red and swollen, and it was difficult to enjoy her society without becoming conscious of a smell of spirits. Like most persons who have attained to great eminence in their profession, she took to hers very kindly; insomuch that, setting aside her natural predilections as a woman, she went to a lying-in or a laying-out with equal zest and relish . . .

'I'm a-going immediate, sir,' returned the nurse; 'unless there's nothing I can do for you, ma'am. Ain't there,' said Mrs Gamp, with a look of great sweetness, and rummaging all the time in her pocket; 'ain't there nothing I can do for you, my little bird?'

'No,' said Merry, almost crying. 'You had better go away, please!'

With a leer of mingled sweetness and slyness; with one eye on the future, one on the bride, and

an arch expression in her face, partly spiritual, partly spirituous, and wholly professional and peculiar to her art; Mrs Gamp rummaged in her pocket again, and took from it a printed card, whereon was an inscription copied from her sign-board.

'Would you be so good, my darling dovey of a dear young married lady,' Mrs Gamp observed, in a low voice, 'as put that somewheres where you can keep it in your mind? I'm well be-known to many ladies, and it's my card. Gamp is my name, and Gamp my nater. Livin' quite handy, I will make so bold as call in now and then, and make inquiry how your health and spirits is, my precious chick!'

And with innumerable leers, winks, coughs, nods, smiles and curtseys, all leading to the establishment of a mysterious and confidential understanding between herself and the bride, Mrs Gamp, invoking a blessing upon the house, leered, winked, coughed, nodded, smiled, and curtseyed herself out of the room.

*Martin Chuzzlewit*,
Charles Dickens

In the hope of speeding up delivery women have been shaken, held upside down and tossed up and down in their blankets. Massage of the abdomen was common, as well as the administration of sneezing powders and drinks of juniper twigs and berries.

The ringing of bells dates back to medieval times when it was thought to induce the saints to help bring forth the child. In Portugal, where the practice continued into the late nineteenth century, the ringing had to be done by nine virgins, each one named Mary, who had to ring out nine peals on the church bells, holding the rope between their teeth at the same time.

In rural communities in Japan, a doll would be brought into the birthing room and used to mimic the birth process in the hopes of encouraging the woman in labour. In China puppets were used for the same purpose.

Around the world, from Papua New Guinea to Korea, one of the most common methods of giving birth is that of crouching or squatting. The woman is usually supported by ropes or straps suspended from the ceiling of the room, or between two trees. Other women hold her, while the midwife waits at her feet to catch the child. The birthing chair was known in ancient times and it remained one of the most popular methods of giving birth until the nineteenth century. In Europe in the eighteenth century when beds became more affordable and available to the general populace, they were put to obvious use in childbirth, although a woman might move to lie on a straw-bedded floor if she possessed only one pair of sheets, which was known as being 'in the straw'. Special mattresses, which could be rolled into different positions around a woman, were available in the eighteenth century. At this time, English and American women were thought to have preferred giving birth on their sides, with the midwife waiting on the bed behind them.

The presence of the father in the delivery room would not be an unusual sight in some societies which permit men to participate in either a symbolic or literal sense. An African tribesman may dig up roots which he is obliged to suck during his wife's delivery. In another tribe, a brother-in-law, or some other male family member – except husbands or brothers – holds on to the woman's nose and breathes into her mouth. Because of the isolation of the Polar Eskimos, the husband helps his wife in labour by placing his arms around her middle and applying pressure. Once the child is born he will continue pressing until the afterbirth emerges.

Most men waited in an ante-room, within uncomfortable, but easy reach.

*An early fourteenth-century bed and cradle in which a waddled baby can be seen*

Traditionally royal births took place in front of a crowd, as in the case of the birth of Louis XIV in 1638, when not only was the royal *accoucheur* present, but also a number of doctors and midwives, as well as a great many members of the court. The presence of a male, other than the doctor, had a lot to do with the practice, since ancient times, of surreptitiously placing a newborn infant into the bed of a barren woman who had deceived her husband with a false pregnancy.

These babies became known as 'warming-pan' babies in the eighteenth century. Midwives, who would be in a position to know who was shortly due to give birth to a child, as well as who wanted a child but couldn't have one,

were usually involved and some midwives carried bullock's blood with them to spread around so that a suspicious husband would be deceived. There were rumours that a baby boy had been smuggled, in a warming pan, into the birthing room of James II's queen. After this, the Home Secretary was expected to attend the birth of a royal child and wait just outside the door. King George VI was the first king since that time to discontinue the practice.

In the seventeenth century the Chamberlen brothers, two men-midwives, were rumoured to be fast and successful in childbirth deliveries. Their methods were kept secret from the public for almost one hundred years, during which time they, and their followers, became popular. They would attend births only if they could be alone with the mother in the room so that no one would see them using forceps, metal blades which they had bound with leather in order to muffle and therefore disguise the instrument. The use of the forceps not only speeded up delivery but generally did less damage to the child than the other instruments in common use at the time.

By the following century the man-midwife attended a birth carrying a bag containing forceps, craniotomy scissors, hooks, knives and other tools associated with his trade. He became known, amongst the fashionable, as an 'accoucheur', a word borrowed from the French, and many midwives who hoped to attract a better-paying client styled themselves as 'accoucheuses' to distinguish themselves from their competitors.

During both the eighteenth and nineteenth centuries 'baby doctors', although they were not known by this name at first, became fashionable amongst the wealthy. The expectant mother was usually brought from her country home to London for the birth. In the case of royalty, women would travel hundreds of miles in order to have their child born in the appropriate country.

While many women continued about their daily business until right up to the time contractions started, most took up residence in their house, or one rented from someone else, several weeks prior to the expected date, with a retinue of servants. Amongst them would be a 'monthly' nurse who would stay with the mother for the first month after the birth, and, if the husband so desired, a wet nurse. Straw was placed outside the house in order to muffle the sounds of footsteps on the street outside.

The doctor engaged to attend the birth of a baby to wealthy parents was faced with a large number of problems. First of all he was obliged to consider

his patient's modesty. Obstetrical students, many of whom received instruction from midwives, were nonetheless taught to avoid touching or looking at the mother and to deliver the child discreetly beneath the bed covers. It was the nineteenth century before the presence of men in the birthing room was really accepted. In 1646 a man in the American state of Maine was prosecuted for acting as a midwife, and in 1772 the *Virginia Gazette* announced that male midwifery was immoral. Many women gave birth fully clothed, wrapped in thin robes to conceal themselves from the doctor. The sacque was a convenient garment, being worn both indoors and out, its shape helping to disguise a prominent abdomen. The bed used was often a special kind of cot, rather than the marriage bed which symbolically related the birthing process to sex, something the Victorians especially tried to avoid.

Secondly, the doctor had to consider the husband. Several doctors were threatened and later charged with adultery by their patients' husbands, and many doctors chose to deliver a child in the presence of a nurse.

The arrival of the doctor in the birthing room signalled the moment when all the other female relatives disappeared. The doctor would stay on call, often being put up in the house, until the woman actually gave birth. If she went into labour and subsequently gave birth before the doctor could be summoned, the nurse was supposed to be capable of delivering the baby.

The idea of having a special doctor attend the birth of a child was well accepted by the aristocracy by the early 1800s. A number of doctors received baronetcies, but other medical men scoffed that these men were more skilled in bedside manners than childbirth practices.

The rise in popularity of the 'baby doctor' may have something to do with the pain-killers he brought with him to the delivery room. When Queen Victoria, in labour with Prince Leopold, took chloroform for the first time in 1853, the drug was provided by Queen's physician, Sir John Snow. Chloroform had been discovered in 1831 by the Scottish physician Sir James Simpson, the New York chemist, Samuel Guthrie, the Parisian Eugène Souberain and J. von Liebig, the German chemist; all of whom were credited with the discovery of the anaesthetic. It was named chloroform four years later. Queen Victoria described the drug as 'blessed chloroform' and found its effect to be 'quieting and delightful beyond measure', despite the disapproval of the medical journal *The Lancet*. In France chloroform became known as '*anaesthésie à la reine*', and by 1857 it was in general use.

The Dispensary Doctor – West of Ireland *by the American painter Howard Helmick (1845–1907)*

Many people were against the use of drugs, as they believed it was the duty of a woman to suffer, particularly in childbirth, and that the pain was a form of expression of love for the as yet unborn child. Women were expected to suffer and James VI of Scotland had Agnes Sampson tried for heresy when she sought relief from pain in labour. She was later thought to be a witch and burned at the stake. Regardless of the idea that women were supposed to bear the pain of childbirth as part of their lot in life, women have always sought methods of relief. The desire for an untroubled childbirth is universal. Herbal mixtures were administered, usually belladonna or ergot, ladies' bedstraw or birthwort, but it is only recently that pain-killers have been found which are both effective and safe.

Although the British Obstetrics Society was founded in 1858, and the American Association of Obstetrics and Gynecologists in 1888, it has been estimated that by the mid-nineteenth century about three quarters of all births in Britain and the USA were still being attended by midwives in the home of the mother. A number of the larger hospitals in England had established beds for teaching obstetrics in the late nineteenth century, but it wasn't until the 1920s that 'baby doctors' were leaving medical schools in any numbers.

French midwives often learned midwifery at the famous Hôtel Dieu in Paris. Founded in AD 650 the Hôtel Dieu's maternity wards were run for twelve hundred years by the Augustine sisters. Although in conception, the maternity, or lying-in, wards were the forerunners of our own modern maternity wards, the comparison stops there, for the incidence of infant mortality and death in childbirth in these wards was enormous. Little was known until the nineteenth century about the passage of infection and many women died here, and elsewhere, of puerperal (childbed) fever.

*A woodcut of 1513 shows a woman giving birth on a low chair: the midwife is ready to receive the child, while another woman supports the mother*

'Lying-in' hospitals devoted exclusively to mothers-to-be and infants were not generally established until the seventeenth century throughout Europe. The care of pregnant women, which we take for granted today, was non-existent until this century. A woman might be bled once or twice during her pregnancy, blood-letting being the most common form of treatment until the last century, but she would receive no other attention. When physicians realized the connections between the health of the mother and the health of her unborn child, centres were established so that by the 1920s in England, for example, women could receive health care.

Childbirth became institutionalized in the first half of this century and, for

a time, women who chose to have their children at home, without the attendant nurses, doctors and injections, were viewed as decidedly old-fashioned. But the baby care of the 1950s was geared more towards the hospital's routines than the individual requirements of mother and baby. Thirty years later, in the 1980s, a woman can choose where and how she wants her baby, and some doctors in the USA will even oblige with 'when', booking a woman who is to be induced into hospital at a time convenient to her schedule. Home births, hospital deliveries with full use of technology, hospital deliveries with the whole family watching and the technology and staff on hand in case of necessity, Lamaze or Leboyer methods – there have never been so many choices of childbirth delivery. And the choice doesn't end there. In America, a prospective mother can select from a number of packages offered by hospitals which include, amongst other things, lobster dinners *à deux* before riding home with baby in a limousine.

It is interesting to note that, in many instances, women are assuming once more responsibilities for themselves in childbirth. Increasing numbers of female doctors are specializing in obstetrics, and many of the available books on childbirth and pregnancy are written by women. Midwives are fast gaining a much-deserved, renewed respectability, and they are now viewed as a viable option in childbirth, generally with the hospital on hand in case of an emergency. Perhaps the important role of the midwife will now be acknowledged, however unscientifically it came into being.

Lully, lulla, thou little tiny child,
By, by, lully, lullay, thou little
tiny child,
By, by, lully, lullay!
*The Coventry Carol*

# Outfitting the Baby

REFLECTION ON BABIES

A bit of talcum
Is always walcum.

           Ogden Nash

'MANY a young mother preparing for her first baby is very puzzled to know exactly what clothes to get ready, not only as to the number of the different garments necessary, but more especially as to the style to be chosen,' wrote Ethel A. Moon, Principal of the well-known Babies Hotel and Nursery Training School of Buxted Lodge, in a February 1926 issue of *The Nursery World*. Ms. (her title was not indicated) Moon was right. Every young mother concerns herself with a layette for the child.

The word layette means different things in different parts of the world. To some people it is strictly the clothing purchased, or made, for the baby; to others it includes blankets, sheets and cot covers; while yet a third group considers that nursery furniture – high-chairs and potties, for example – to be part of the layette.

In earlier centuries, the creation of a layette was thought to be a suitable occupation for the mother during the latter stages of her pregnancy when she was prohibited from doing much else. Before the sewing machine came into use everything had to be stitched by hand, a time-consuming process, and probably the reason why so many clothes were passed on from one woman to another and from one generation to the next. Some working-class women in eighteenth-century England formed a club to which they contributed 6*d*. of their income, which was used to purchase infant clothing. New mothers belonging to the club could borrow these items for their newborn child, returning the clothes once the infant had grown out of them, or if the baby died, so that another mother might make use of the garments.

Before the days of central heating, infants needed to be well protected from the cold. Most infants were swaddled from birth, the swaddling bands being made of strips of linen or cotton, but gradually infants began to wear clothing, initially underneath their swaddling clothes, but alone after the eighteenth century when swaddling went out of fashion.

The extent of the layette would depend very much on the funds available to the mother, but layering seemed to be the order of the day, until the second half of this century when infants are allowed more freedom than ever before. Surprisingly enough, fashions in infant clothing changed remarkably little over the centuries. The names of seventeenth- and eighteenth-century garments are unfamiliar to us, but they have similar uses to garments in the nineteenth and even the early twentieth centuries.

Fashion, of course, played its part, but not in terms of decoration and style – that came much later – but in the manner in which a baby was dressed and the fabrics used.

Although no specific layette exists for a baby born in the late sixteenth century, midwives were recommended to provide, soap, candles and swaddling bands with headbands and crosscloths, in case the mother's supply was insufficient. The midwife might expect to find laid out for her by the 'gossips' who assisted at a birth biggins (bonnets) for the baby's head, as no baby went bare-headed, bibs, tailclouts (nappies) which were often made from the husband's old shirts, mantles (cloaks), hose (some sort of knitted hose was likely), wastcoats (waistcoats, a sleeveless coat buttoning or tying at the front), shirts (shifts), petticoats and shoes.

Items supplied to each new admission at Thomas Coram's Foundling Hospital in London in 1741 were: four linnen biggens (bonnets); four linnen stays (laced corset-like objects); four linnen caps (often to be worn under the bonnet); four linnen neck cloths (small shawls perhaps?); four linnen shirts and twelve linnen clouths (nappies or diapers); one grey linsey mantle (woollen cloak); a pair of grey linsey sleeves (woollen sleeves); two white bays blankettes; one rowle; and two doubles pilches (over-pants worn over the clouths).

When swaddling was no longer considered appropriate for infants in the nineteenth century, binders were used. These long narrow clothes were designed to be worn around the baby's stomach in order to keep the umbilical cord dressing in place, and to keep the baby warm. Binders, belts or body

belts as they were known were still in use in the early twentieth century. Flannel binders were used initially, but after the first two weeks, knitted or woven belts – many of them had shoulder straps and a small tab at the end for pinning napkins to – were favoured. Not everyone was keen on body belts: some mothers and nurses thought that infants stood more chances of catching cold with them than without them.

The most noticeable difference between nineteenth- and early twentieth-century layettes is the absence of so many layers in the later years, and the decreased number of caps and bonnets. In the twentieth century people realized that infants would not die if their bare heads were revealed to the world. Nurses in the 1920s deplored the use of the linen shift followed by layers of petticoats and finally a starched and embroidered robe that were the hallmarks of the well-dressed nineteenth-century baby. In the 1920s vests were worn under a petticoat and gown, which was changed after three months for a jersey and leggings, much more like the modern baby of today.

For night-time instead of a completely different, and just as cumbersome, outfit worn by the nineteenth-century baby, the baby in the 1920s and 1930s wore a Viyella or wincey nightgown which did not resist his or her leg movements.

A great deal was written about napkins (nappies), or diapers as they are also known. Most were made of Turkish towelling which was washed, boiled and washed time and again for successive children, although butter-muslin squares – Harrington Squares as they were known – were also in use. Towelling was, of course, a much later invention, and some parents felt that it was not sufficiently soft enough for baby's bottom, preferring instead to use two Harringtons, although these could not be boiled in the same way as towelling nappies.

Curiously enough, in the age of disposables, some mothers are turning back the clock and have joined a 'Nappy' or 'Diaper' Service whereby clean, boiled articles are delivered daily to their homes and the soiled ones taken away.

According to Phyllis Cunnington and Catherine Lucas in their book *Costume for Births, Marriages and Deaths* published in 1972, a layette in the 1840s comprised of:

4 long nightgowns

4 first day caps

5 long robes

4 day gowns for first month

8 pinafores

2 doz. napkins

3 flannel barrows

9 back wrappers

4 flannel belts or soft calico binders

3 whittles (large white shawls)

6 first-sized shirts

2 flannel caps

2 short chemises

Baby linen, basket and cover

Powder box, pin cushion

Soft sponge and soft brush for the hair.

In her book *Royal Children* (published in 1981) Celia Clear writes that in 1864 Princess Alexandra was pregnant with her first child. She went unexpectedly into labour one afternoon and Lady Macclesfield, the lady of the bed chamber, had to rush out and buy a layette from the local drapers. The layette consisted of:

2 yards of coarse flannel

6 yards of superfine flannel

1 sheet of wadding (lent by Mrs Knollys)

1 basket (contents wanting)

1 superb lace christening robe

The Army & Navy Stores Catalogue of 1907 recommends the following items of merchandise for the expectant mother:

| Item | Price | £ | s | d |
|---|---|---|---|---|
| 6 Lawn Shirts | 1/9 | £0 | 10 | 6 |
| 3 „ „ | 2/8 | 0 | 8 | 0 |
| 4 Woven Linen Swathes | 0/8½ | 0 | 2 | 10 |
| 3 Flannel Swathes | 0/8½ | 0 | 2 | 1½ |
| 4 Night Flannels | 0/10 | 0 | 7 | 4 |
| 4 Day „ | 3/4 | 0 | 13 | 4 |
| 6 Night Gowns | 3/0 | 0 | 18 | 0 |
| 3 Day „ | 4/6 | 0 | 13 | 6 |
| 3 „ „ | 5/9 | 0 | 17 | 3 |
| 3 Doz. Linen Towels | 10/6 | 1 | 11 | 6 |
| 6 Flannel Pilches | 1/2 | 0 | 7 | 0 |
| 2 Waterproof „ | 1/2 | 0 | 2 | 4 |
| 4 Pairs Wool Boots | 1/0 | 0 | 4 | 0 |
| 4 Fancy Bibs | 1/0 | 0 | 4 | 0 |
| 2 „ „ | 1/6 | 0 | 3 | 0 |
| 4 Long Slips | 3/8 | 0 | 14 | 8 |
| 1 Embroidered Head Flannel | | 0 | 8 | 9 |
| 1 Robe, trimmed embroidered | | 0 | 14 | 6 |
| 1 „ „ lace | | 1 | 1 | 6 |
| 1 „ „ „ | | 1 | 15 | 6 |
| 1 Cashmere Cloak | | 1 | 10 | 0 |
| 1 Silk Hood | | 1 | 10 | 6 |
| | £14 | | 0 | 1½ |

THE WORLD OF THE BABY

From the London store of Harvey Nichols the following layette is taken from a 1936 catalogue.

*Everything*

*for*

*every*

*Baby*

BABY WEAR

DICKINS AND JONES

| | | | |
|---|---|---|---|
| 6 wrap-over vests | from 3s. | 1 silk matinée jacket | from 16s.6d. |
| 4 long flannels | from 11s.6d. | 6 bibs of hand-embroidered muslin | from 3s.11d. |
| 4 long petticoats | from 6s.11d. | 3 dozen Turkish squares | from 10s.6d. |
| 6 day gowns | from 11s.6d. | 3 dozen Harrington squares | from 13s.9d. |
| 6 cotton nightgowns | from 6s.11d. | 2 pairs of cot blankets | from 7s.11d. |
| 6 Chilprufe nightgowns | from 11s.3d. | 6 linen pillow slips | from 2s.6d. |
| 6 nun's veiling nightgowns | from 8s.6d. | 6 embroidered muslin pillow slips | from 10s.6d. |
| 2 robes, muslin, organdie or net | from 39s.6d. | 1 down quilt, plain or floral | from 12s.11d. |
| 6 hand-knitted wool jackets | from 5s.11d. | Organdie cot trimmings | from 49s.6d. |
| 1 crêpe-de-Chine shawl | from 69s.6d. | Cane basket | from 59s.6d. |
| 1 wool carrying shawl | from 12s.6d. | | |
| 2 light Shetland shawls | from 4s.11d. | | |

Another London store, Dickins & Jones, produced this booklet in 1951, which gives details of a suggested layette.

*A Minimum Layette*

| | | | |
|---|---|---|---|
| Nightdresses | from 10/1 each | | 3 |
| Wrap-over Vests | ,, 3/6 ,, | | 4 |
| Short Dresses | ,, 15/– ,, | | 3 |
| Shawl | ,, 18/3 ,, | | 2 |
| Matinee Jackets | ,, 13/11 ,, | | 3 |
| Bootees | ,, 4/6 | per pair | 2 pairs |
| Mitts | ,, 4/6 | ,, ,, | 2 ,, |
| Turkish Squares | ,, 26/4 | per doz. | 2 doz. |
| Muslin Squares | ,, 21/– | ,, ,, | 1 ,, |

OUTFITTING THE BABY

According to the authors of *The Great American Birth Rite*, William and Joanna Woolfolk (published in New York in 1975), the following list, based on minimum needs, is essential for newborn babies. Prices were average retail in 1974.

| | |
|---|---|
| 6 dozen diapers at $8.50 per dozen | $51.00 |
| 8 cotton undershirts at $1.25 each | $10.00 |
| 4 cotton kimonos at $3.00 each | $12.00 |
| 4 cotton gowns at $3.00 each | $12.00 |
| 4 sacque sets at $4.50 each | $18.00 |
| 4 waterproof panties at $1.75 each | $7.00 |
| 1 sweater set at $8.00 each | $8.00 |
| 3 stretch terry coveralls at $6.00 each | $18.00 |
| 5 receiving blankets at $2.00 each | $10.00 |
| 2 thermal sleepers at $5.00 each | $10.00 |
| 6 pairs of booties or bootie socks at $1.25 each | $7.50 |
| 3 crib blankets at $10.00 each | $30.00 |
| 6 knitted crib sheets at $4.00 each | $24.00 |
| 3 flannelette waterproof sheets at $4.00 each | $12.00 |
| 6 waterproof lap pads (3 for $1.50) | $3.00 |
| 1 comforter or quilt at $12.00 | $12.00 |
| 2 heavyweight outdoor or travel wraps at $15.00 each | $30.00 |
| Miscellaneous | $35.00 |
| TOTAL | $309.50 |
| Stroller | $50.00 |
| Crib | $100.00 |
| Crib mattress | $30.00 |
| Crib bumpers | $10.00 |
| Infant seat (to carry baby) | $12.00 |
| Chest of drawers | $80.00 |
| Nurery lamp | $20.00 |
| Playpen | $50.00 |
| High-chair or Feeding table | $50.00 |
| Bassinet | $50.00 |
| Diaper Pail | $5.00 |
| Baby Swing | $25.00 |
| Car seat | $35.00 |

These total $517, making a combined total of $826.50.

In those sections of the country where a baby carriage is used, that would cost an additional $100 or more. In rural areas or in cities where the automobile is the principal means of transportation, however, car seats are more popular and baby carriages are regarded as luxury items.

The No-Frills Shopping List: what to get year by year. This is taken from *The Mother to Mother Baby Care Book* by Barbara Sills and Jeanne Henry, published in 1981.

## *Birth to 1 Year*

**BABY LINEN,**

| | | |
|---|---|---|
| List No. 1 | ... | .. £5 5 6 |
| List No. 2 | ... | ... 11 2 3 |
| List No. 3 | ... | ... 25 11 8 |
| List No. 4 | ... | ... 47 6 9 |
| List No. 5* | ... | ... 31 0 4 |

* A specialité for hot climates.

" Excellent quality and good taste."—Queen.

*Clothing and Bedding*

*Diapers (4 dozen prefolded cloth diapers and 3 boxes of disposables per week)*

*Pins (if plastic-head, should be metal lined)*

Bedding
3 fitted crib sheets
2 crib-size mattress pads
1 plastic crib mattress protector
2 crib-size rubber sheets
2 small washable quilts
1 set bumper pads for crib
6 lap-size flannelized rubber
   pads

*Infant Clothes*
6 undershirts (the side-snap kind is
   easier to put on)
1 newborn-size stretch suit (in which to
   take baby home from hospital)
6 stretch suits (6–12 month size)
6 gowns (with drawstring bottoms)
1 hat
3 small plastic or cloth bibs

4 receiving blankets
6 waterproof pants (if you use cloth
   diapers)
1 bunting or snowsuit (depending on
   climate)
2 sets of bootees

*Crawler clothes*
6 pairs overalls (with snap crotch)
6 tops
6 undershirts (depending on climate)
1 sweater
1 jacket with hood (depending on
   climate)
2 blanket sleepers

*Furniture*
Crib and mattress
Bassinet, cradle or car bed
Portable crib (optional)
High-chair or feeding table
Playpen and pad
Changing table
Chest of drawers (or shelves)
Plastic diaper pail with cover
Rocker with arm support for parents
   (optional)

## OUTFITTING THE BABY

*Mobility aids*

Infant seat
Car restraint for infant
Sling or wrap carrier

Backpack carrier
Diaper bag
Umbrella stroller

From the Mothercare catalogue of spring/summer 1984 comes the following layette.

2 cotton wrapover vests
2 baby's stretch bodysuits with easy-fit envelope neck
2 baby's first all-in-one babystretch
2 winceyette baby gowns
2 matinée jackets
2 hats
2 pairs bootees
2 pairs outdoor mittens
2 pairs scratch mittens
1 baby's first blanket
2 waterproof-backed terry bibs
1 toiletries gift box containing baby powder, baby lotion, baby shampoo and baby soap

1 pack of 12 de-luxe absorbent terry nappies
1 pack of 200 supersoft fabric nappy liners
1 pack of 24 all-in-one disposable nappy and pants
1 pack of 3 Ever-dri nappies
1 card of 6 nappy pins
2 pairs of long-life luxury water-proof pants
1 pack of NSP nappy sanitizing powder

Complete with
presentation gift box    £52.35

*Mother and baby in the 1920s*

*American Baby* magazine reported in 1986 that the average first-year expenses for a new baby were as follows:

| | |
|---|---|
| Nursery | $770 |
| Diapers | $624 |
| Formula | $532 |
| Clothing | $412 |
| Baby food | $273 |
| Camera and film | $222 |
| Toys | $100 |

# The First Need

ONE of the first things babies need when they are born is food. Looking back through history we assume that breast-feeding was the only way in which infants were fed, but closer examination proves that this was not the case. Fashion, social attitudes and the health of the mother are all reasons which made people decide whether their babies should be fed by mother's breast, by a wet nurse or from a bottle on a kind of gruel mixture.

Infant feeding practices in the past were often a matter of life or death. Until fairly recently in history, our diet proved insufficient to the extent that large numbers of people, and particularly babies, died of malnutrition. Even if a mother chose to breast-feed her own baby, and this was by no means as normal as we like to think, her diet, if she was poor, was often inadequate to sustain an infant.

Vegetables were known in Europe since the eighth century but they were not available to everyone and crops did not always survive harsh winters. People lived largely on a diet of meat, bread, fish if they were near a coast or river, and some fruit. Dairy products were rare. Water was looked upon with great suspicion as a carrier of death, poisoned by devils or whichever peoples happened to be out of favour.

Wine or ale was drunk mostly. Strong spirits were available in the cities by the eighteenth century, as the familiar works of the artist William Hogarth depicted, and nursing mothers could be seen drinking gin on the streets.

Milk was not pasteurized until the 1890s and milk from a goat or cow was generally avoided before then, particularly for infants, because people

believed their child would grow up to resemble the animal; although the deified heroes of Roman mythology, Romulus and Remus, sons of the god Mars, were suckled by a she-wolf, and we must assume that this legend had its basis in everyday life. In the nineteenth century it was not uncommon in European foundling hospitals, particularly those in France, for infants to be put under goats' udders when no other form of nourishment could be found.

Mother's milk was subject to strange ideas and beliefs. The Greeks thought that milk was produced in the uterus and transported to the breast by special vessels in the body. There existed since the Middle Ages a vague awareness that breast milk provided some protection against sickness, but colostrum, the fluid secreted after birth, was considered dangerous and women were advised not to feed the newborn baby for a few days. An older child would draw the breast milk first.

In medieval times people thought that breast milk would curdle if the mother did not have an infant to suckle. Unruly children were believed to be the result of inferior breast milk. The Incas were not the only peoples to believe that sex reduced the amount of milk and in many parts of the world sex is forbidden until the child is weaned.

The hygienic sterilized conditions under which we bottle – or formula – feed infants today is taken for granted. In the past people had no idea that germs, harboured in a pap spoon which was kept lukewarm over a fire, could cause sickness and even death. In addition, in the seventeenth century doctors believed that many infant ailments were caused by the presence of too much acid in the stomach. Babies were fed chalk, crushed eggshells, coral and oyster shells, mixed with their gruel, which was intended to counteract the acidity.

What we know about infant feeding practices now has been gathered from available material dating from the seventeenth, eighteenth and nineteenth centuries. Before this time, there was a lack of written data in general and about babies in particular. For centuries childbirth and babies were considered the responsibilities of women: men got involved only when either mother or child became sick. Not every woman knew how to read or write.

The inadequate amount of written material means that we have to rely on surviving objects for information. Tucked away in the storerooms of the world's museums we can find evidence of bottle feeding, 'artificial' feeding as it became known, from ancient times to the present day. We must therefore conclude that both the breast and the bottle were used to feed infants, but it

She was perfectly quiet now, but not asleep – only soothed by sweet porridge and warmth into that wide-gazing calm which makes us older human beings, with our inward turmoil, feel a certain awe in the presence of a little child, such as we feel before some quiet majesty or beauty in the earth or sky – before a steady glowing planet, or a full-flowered eglantine, or the bending trees over a silent pathway.

*Silas Marner*, George Eliot

would be ill-advised to guess at the degree to which one or the other was favoured. Due to the fragile nature and limited use of the feeding bottles, many must have been destroyed once they were no longer required.

How an infant was fed in the past was determined by one, or a combination, of three things: the health of the mother; the economics of the household into which the baby was born; and the attitude of the mother towards breast-feeding and, therefore, the dictates of society at the time.

If a woman did not survive childbirth, or if she was incapable of breast-feeding, then alternatives would have to be found, either in the form of a wet nurse, or by feeding the infant foodstuffs from some kind of vessel.

The history of the wet nurse in society is directly related to the popularity of breast-feeding. In the eighteenth century, for example, well-to-do women were known to get the vapours at the thought of breast-feeding their own children. Wet nurses were in great demand at this time, but by the 1920s, when fashion dictated the slim, gamine shape, many women thought that nursing a baby would make them fat, and they bound their breasts and reached for the sterilized feeding bottle which had, during the course of the previous century, entirely replaced the wet nurse.

Without the use of birth control, a woman might expect to have a large number of children during her lifetime, but many of them would not survive the first few months. The high infant mortality rate meant that a woman who had lost her own child might be able to secure a position as a wet nurse to another woman's child. Alternatively, economics might have forced her to seek employment as a wet nurse, abandoning her own offspring to the care of her older children. While this sounds tragic to us, we must remember that until the nineteenth century babies were not considered to have personalities, and therefore they were not in need of the physical and psychological nurturing advised today. In poor families there might not have been enough food to go round and frequent deaths, while no doubt sad and causing great grief to the mother, must have been accepted as part of life. Indeed, some people believed, and this is especially true of primitive cultures, that the high death rate reflected the role nature played in the survival of the fittest.

A woman hired as a wet nurse to a family would find her status in the world vastly improved. Women found it almost impossible to get paid a living wage, but a wet nurse could be assured of both money and respect. She might be expected to nurse two or three children successively, but she would

be given preferential treatment in the household, eating and drinking as much as she liked. It was not unusual for a wet nurse to take advantage of her situation. There is the story of the revolting Mrs Pack who in 1689 became the wet nurse to the Duke of Gloucester, succeeding where all other wet nurses had failed in keeping the little prince alive with her milk. As a result she was able to do what she liked, which included remaining unwashed, and to eat and drink as much as she wanted. Unwashed wet nurses who were too drunk to suckle their employer's baby were not unusual.

Most wet nurses were recommended within a community. The state of health of a woman's own children was thought to represent the quality of her milk, so no doubt the sickly offspring were concealed and only the healthy were presented to the world.

*French artist Alfred Roll's (1846–1919) painting* The Wet Nurse

Wealthy people, well-to-do merchants and the aristocracy in Europe liked to think that the poor had a plentiful supply of milk. However, wet nurses were chosen with great care because it was believed, at least until the nineteenth century, that babies absorbed the characteristics of the nurse from her milk. Redheaded nurses were avoided for their legendary hot tempers. In addition to a gentle nature, some parents looked for a wet nurse who physically resembled the baby's mother. Other than full, firm breasts full of milk, the wet nurse was also required to have a clear complexion and 'sweet breath', the latter quality being rather hard to find in the days before regular dental check-ups.

Religion played its part: in 1235 Henry III decreed that Christian wet nurses could not suckle Jews.

Rewards for a wet nurse who successfully nursed a favoured son of a prominent family, or even a king's son, were not unusual; as her reputation increased so did her power and situation. In the 1730s a wet nurse in a wealthy family might expect to earn 100 guineas a year, plus board and lodging.

Throughout the eighteenth century writers on obstetrics and paediatrics, who were, almost without exception, men, berated well-to-do women for not breast-feeding their own children. This was nothing new. Since the fourteenth century, and possibly even earlier, men accused women of neglecting their maternal duties, preferring instead to 'frolic' with their husbands.

Husbands did indeed play a role in the hired-versus-mother's-own debate. Some men, resenting sleepless nights and the intrusions of a hungry child in

**Feeding Bottles, Teats, and Fittings**

Boat Shape Feeding Bottle,
each 0/5

Maw's old-fashioned Feeders (screw glass stopper and teat attached), each, 0/7½, 0/8, 0/9½

Spare Bottles for do. ... each 0/3½, 0/4  0/5
„ Stoppers „ ..................... each 0/2½

"Alexandra," with glass screw stopper, each ......... 1/0

Spare bottles for do., each ......... 0/4

**The "Army & Navy" Improved Hygienic Feeding Bottle.**

Advantages — Having no corners, can be readily cleaned by simply flushing direct from the tap. No rubber tubing required, therefore one cause of constant trouble removed. Is graduated so as to be able to register quantity of food. Has an outside air valve, thus doing away with necessity of neck in which sour milk secretes itself.

Each ........................... complete in box  0/9½
Extra teats, each 0/2½ ; extra valves, each  0/2
The "Allenburys" Feeder, complete in cardboard box ........................ each  1/2
Spare Teats ...... ....................... „  0/4
  „  Valves................ ........... „  0/3
  „  Bottles ...... .................. „  0/9

*The 1907 Army & Navy catalogue offered a variety of feeding bottles, teats, fittings and milk sterilising kits*

their bedrooms, ordered a wet nurse for their offspring, regardless of whether or not their wife wanted to breast-feed, and this continued until the nineteenth century when a woman became less the chattel of her husband, expected to carry out his every wish. Queen Caroline, wife of King George II, was praised for nursing her own children, but wet nurses were included amongst the royal staff.

By the 1800s, however, despite the urgings of writers of child-care, numerous infants were still being nursed by wet nurses. Advertisements appeared in *The Times* for wet nurses, right up to the 1880s, when the practice of wet nursing declined.

It is easy to believe in the idea that modernization was responsible for the swing in the late nineteenth century from the breast-feeding of babies to bottle or formula feeding. By this time new technology in manufacturing processes had resulted in better products, and the expansion of the railways meant that cow's milk, now far freer of bacteria than ever before, could be distributed with greater speed. But the truth is that the nineteenth century was really no different from any other period, for since early times women have found alternative ways of feeding their own babies, and when wet nurses went out of fashion, formulas were in. The word 'formula' was used from about 1700 when it was taken to mean a recipe or prescription. From the mid-nineteenth century it was used in a scientific context. Later, it was appropriated by manufacturers of baby foods and it is now a generic term used in the USA to describe milk fed to infants by bottle.

It is impossible to know what Greeks or Romans fed their babies on, or even those in the Middle Ages, but we do know that in the eighteenth century many babies were brought up on a kind of gruel, made of flour and water. Known variously as pap, panada, or a caudle, this unhealthy mixture which, when kept warm, was a breeding ground for bacteria, most closely resembled wallpaper paste. Depending on economics, the gruel was also made of mixtures of wine or beer or cow's milk instead of water, and bread or oatmeal instead of flour, with added spices. Babies were also fed cake, moistened meal and sweetmeats. Until the early twentieth century people thought nothing about giving sluggish babies stimulants such as tea, coffee and wine, while over-excitable babies were thought to benefit from what were considered the calming effects of eggs and vegetables. No one paid any attention to the idea of constipation, and calories did not feature until this century.

*Expectation: Interior of a Cottage by Frederick Daniel Hardy (1826–1911). Paintings of rural life and cottage scenes were enormously popular in the nineteenth century, corresponding with the upper-class view of the peasant's world*

THE FIRST NEED

Caudle was also given to expectant mothers and invalids and would have been made of spiced wine and oatmeal. It was originally served in a posset pot but later it became a two-handled cup with a cover and a saucer. Caudle cups were generally made of pewter, but elaborate caudle cups made of silver were included as part of a tea service.

Spoons were often used to feed infants. They were known as pap boats, and expensive and elaborate versions were made by silversmiths for those who could afford it. The expression 'to be born with a silver spoon in one's mouth' most probably evolved around the sixteenth century, although spoons have always played an important part in history. In earlier times, on social visits, one would be expected to take one's own spoon to the home of the hosts. Cutlery in general was not plentiful, and spoons were precious gifts, given at christenings and weddings. By the 1600s a kind of travelling spoon was being made, two spoons at either end of a handle.´

The pap spoon, or boat as it was called, was far larger than a regular spoon, with a long curved handle. It was covered with a lid which could be raised so that the pap could be put inside. The spout was curved to fit the baby's mouth. Other feeding spoons were made of pewter, earthenware or porcelain.

*Some feeding vessels were highly decorated, such as this glazed and transfer-printed earthenware feeding bottle made c. 184(. The hole at the top would have been stuffed with rags or a cork to prevent the contents from spilling*

Feeding vessels were made in all shapes and sizes. Horn was used as an early drinking vessel for adults and must therefore have been employed for babies. Athenian feeding bottles, made of clay, were designed rather like jugs with a handle on one side. On the other side was a spout upon which the child sucked and the food, whatever that might have been, was strained through a sieve-like device in the neck.

The common element of all feeding vessels was a tubular shape with a place for the infant to suck, which was necessarily smaller than the place where the foodstuff was admitted. This hole had to be plugged, and on glass and ceramic bottles corks were often used, or the hole would be stuffed with rags.

In the eighteenth century pewter nursing bottles were used. Some versions had screw tops, and resembled bulbous salt cellars with screw-on nipples. Spouted feeders, which looked rather like coffee pots, were made with a rounded spout on to which a nipple could be attached. In this way the foodstuff could be almost poured into the infant's mouth.

In India, where wet nurses were rarely used, boat-shaped bottles made of brass were available for women who couldn't feed their own infants.

*Athenian feeding bottle with a filter at the top, a handle and a spout*

Glass was also used to create feeding vessels in the past but very few examples of the hand-blown variety have survived. Glass feeding bottles were being mass-produced by the nineteenth century. Many of them were submarine-shaped with the nipple being an integral part of the bottle. Despite the fact that they contributed to a great number of infant deaths, glass bottles were by far the most popular method of feeding babies in the nineteenth century. The long tube nursing bottle was in wide use and was the major culprit as the carrier of disease. The flat bottle, into which the long tube was inserted, could be placed alongside the baby in a crib. The tube, with a nipple on the end, extended some way out of the bottle so that it reached the baby's mouth. Although special brushes were sold which were supposed to clean the apparatus, these tubes were rarely and inadequately washed, which provided bacteria with a perfect breeding ground.

Bottles were sold by apothecaries and, later, chemists, but in the early twentieth century they could be purchased, along with other infant parapher-nalia such as nipple shields, nipples, nursery bottle fittings and breast pumps, by mail through, for example, the Sears, Roebuck catalogue in the USA, the Army and Navy catalogue in the UK and other mail-order stores.

*A collection of nursery appliances, including a breast-exhauster (pump), nipple shields and dress protector*

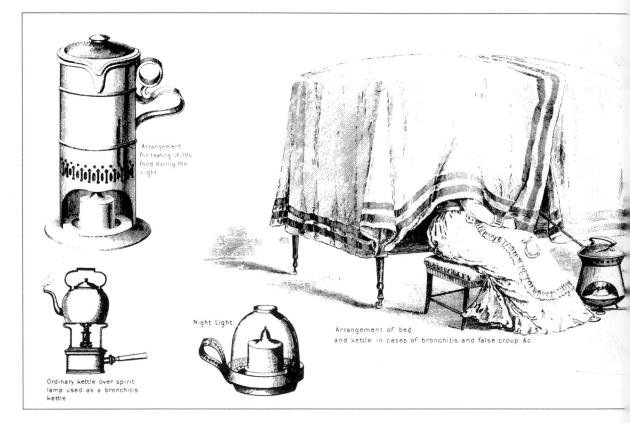

Arrangement for heating child's food during the night.

Ordinary kettle over spirit lamp used as a bronchitis kettle.

Night Light.

Arrangement of bed and kettle in cases of bronchitis and false croup &c.

In 1845 a rubber nipple was patented in the USA by Elijah Pratt. However, nipples at this time did not help the infant in any way as they were not sterilized and were, quite possibly, used by more than one member of the family. Before the invention of rubber, nipples for feeding bottles were made of chamois, leather, parchment, or a thin woven linen or gauze. Calf's teats were treated with spirits, and even decalcified ivory was used.

Nipple shields, designed to prevent or protect cracked nipples, were in use from the seventeenth century. Some were made of wood, and later rubber. The rubber nipples were placed over them. Nipple shells, usually made of glass, were attached to the breast so that milk could be trapped inside where it wouldn't soak the mother's clothing. Breast pumps came into use in the second half of the nineteenth century. Many were made of glass and they

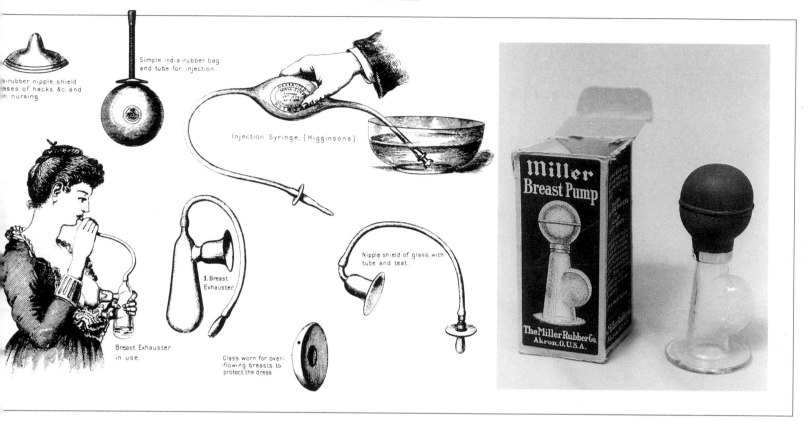

-rubber nipple shield
ases of hacks &c. and
n nursing.

Simple india-rubber bag
and tube for injection

Injection Syringe. (Higginsons).

Breast Exhauster
in use.

1. Breast
Exhauster.

Glass worn for over-
-flowing breasts to
protect the dress

Nipple shield of glass, with
tube and teat.

*The American-made Miller Breast Pump*

were designed to be attached to the breast, a long handle allowing the mother to draw off the milk herself by mouth. Later, cylindrical tubes came into use. These had a bulbous space on one side for collecting the milk, and a rubber bulb which could be squeezed to provide suction at the end.

In the second half of the nineteenth century pap was replaced by cow's milk amongst those who could afford to purchase it. But it was not until the early twentieth century that commissions were established to certify cow's milk. Although cow's milk had been analysed in 1799 it was not properly understood until the 1860s when scientists developed a 'formula' for changing cow's milk so that it resembled mother's milk. These 'formulas' of the 1850s and 1860s were extremely complicated to prepare, sometimes requiring the use of algebra, and it is no accident that their appearance coincided with the

modernization of the household. Piped hot water began to be available to homes in the second half of the nineteenth century. Another factor to be considered was the widespread use of nurses amongst the wealthy, which freed mother from the time-consuming duties of preparing the formula.

Condensed, evaporated and dehydrated cow's milk appeared on shelves alongside canned foods and various formulas. These items were available for purchase at stores and through advertisements in magazines. In the 1880s Nestlés and Horlick's were well-known milk-like foods made of dried cow's milk with added cereal and sugar. Mellin's was a malted preparation much favoured by doctors, while Eskay's and Imperial Granum were cereals designed to be used with fresh cow's milk. 'Mincasea' was just one of many products available which claimed to be able to transform cow's milk into breast milk. Many of these canned foodstuffs made wild claims as to their efficacy. Doctors endorsed some products by attaching their names to the advertisements. Today, some of these manufacturers, and certainly the doctors, would be brought before the advertising standards watchdogs, and in the USA law suits by the thousand would be pending, but one hundred years ago women readily purchased these products and fed them to their offspring.

In the eighteenth century few upper-class women breast-fed their own babies, preferring instead the services of a wet nurse. In the following century the wet nurse was replaced by artificial foodstuffs, as they were known. Queen Victoria did not like breast-feeding and did not breast-feed her nine children for long. But by the 1900s more women were breast-feeding their own children. They were encouraged to be as docile as possible, rather like cows, and to avoid all forms of excitement, especially sexual excitement. Novels were also thought to arouse dangerous levels of excitement which would have an effect on the quality and quantity of milk produced.

Strained baby food was available by prescription from doctors in the early twentieth century. Daniel Gerber, who worked with his father at the Fremont Canning Company, strained some peas for his sickly daughter in the late 1920s and found an alternative feeding method. By the 1930s strained baby foods, in tins or jars, mostly fruit or vegetable based, were available.

In the past, fashions in breast-feeding were cyclical and had by no means stabilized even in the twentieth century. In the USA, only 38 per cent of babies were breast-fed in 1946, and twenty years later this figure had dropped to 23 per cent.

*Paul César Helleu's (1859–1927) tender portrait of his wife and their daughter Ellen*

MATERNAL LOVE

The Fashionable Mama
or The Convenience of
Modern Dress, *an
eighteenth-century
engraving by James Gillray,
contrasts the mother's
costume and attitude with
that of the portrait in the
background*

## THE FIRST NEED

After the social upheaval of the First World War with the resulting changes in society, nurses and nannies were no longer permanent fixtures of middle- and upper-class homes. This left mother, quite literally, holding the baby. The breast-is-best campaign received a shot in the arm in 1917 when Truby King visited Britain from his native New Zealand. He was a strong advocate of breast-feeding on a regular planned schedule. The Mothercraft School was established in Highgate, London, to promote breast-feeding and other methods of bringing up babies.

In the early part of this century increasing amounts of literature were published on infant care and management. Much of this discussed the best methods of feeding infants, from feeding on demand to the adherence to scheduled feeds when babies were fed strictly by the book, regardless of his or her size and weight. To some people a crying baby was a hungry baby and therefore should be fed; others believed that breaking a baby's feeding schedule would encourage bad habits later in life. Mothers were strongly advised to avoid certain foodstuffs, especially fruits with pips in them, and to avoid drinking alcohol, although it is now considered fashionable for a nursing mother to drink a glass of ale or stout. Successive generations reject the ideas of the preceding generation. Anyone who has picked up a contemporary child-care manual will be familiar with the debates.

Although we have done a great deal in the twentieth century to reduce drastically the infant mortality rate, we should not expect people, two hundred years from now, to find our methods and ideas concerning infant feeding practices to be adequate for their time.

*Ancient boat-shaped feeding bottle made of black glazed terracotta. Vessels similar to these were still in use in the eighteenth century*

# Swaddling

The practice of swaddling babies – wrapping them in bands of fabric – is centuries old. Swaddling bands were long strips of fabric, usually made of linen or cotton, which were wound around and around the baby rather like the bindings on an Egyptian mummy. There were a number of ways in which to swaddle the baby: evidence of this can be found in ancient art which shows women holding these tiny bundles packaged in a number of styles, with bands going cross-ways or criss-cross.

Historians have argued that babies were swaddled to protect them from cold temperatures: the extra heat of the swaddling bands had the additional benefit of helping to induce sleep in the child. The material also provided some degree of padding if the child was attacked by a wild animal, and the swaddled child who was left alone for hours could be prevented from hurting himself. In the days before disposable nappies, swaddling clothes masked the need for the baby to be changed frequently.

A further justification for swaddling came from the belief that children could not grow tall and strong without the assistance of bands to bind their limbs, bodies and, in some cases, their heads, into position. Cultures in Africa, North and South America and Europe have indulged in skull moulding, in which a variety of tight bindings and squeezing boards are used to create a desired shape. The most universally popular head shape was that of a flattened forehead with a tapering, pointed crown. High heads could not carry burdens. Ancient Egyptians believed that the shape of the head influenced intelligence and they squashed the heads of newborns to balloon out at the back of the skull. This shape was still popular in France until the last century.

But the real objective in swaddling babies was to make them conform to adult requirements from the moment they were born. A swaddled baby was easier to handle than one who was kicking and flailing about. A wrapped bundle was less of a burden when he or she could be placed in a makeshift cradle, or even suspended from a peg, well out of harm's way.

By Tudor times infants were wearing clothing under their swaddling bands. Most often these clothes consisted of a long- or short-sleeved shirt or shift with lace-trimmed sleeves and, depending on current fashions, a collar or ruff, a 'tailclout' (nappy/diaper) and a decorative 'crosseclothe', made from a triangular piece of fabric which was lace-trimmed on one side and tied underneath the chin. The 'biggin' (cap) went on over the crosseclothe allowing the lace to show beneath. Some babies also wore mittens and bibs. Swaddling bands were placed over the clothing, either encasing the arms or, depending on the age of the child and the fashions of the time, allowing the arms to be left free.

Two hundred years ago a peasant woman would swaddle her baby by sitting herself down on the ground with her legs stretched out in front of her. Her baby would be placed between her legs with her feet and toes supporting its head. The first strip of fabric was tied around the child's head. The next piece, folded into a triangle, was wrapped around the upper torso of the child and fastened under the armpits. The third piece, the largest yet, covered the child from neck to feet and was wrapped under the child. The last binding was made of a long narrow strip which was wound around and around the baby, securing the other pieces of fabric, until two short ends were left. These were often used to tie the baby's hands or feet together.

If swaddling failed to immobilize the baby, some parents tied or laced their offspring into a cradle or crib. Obviously, the laces created the need for knobs on the cradle around which they could be tied. When swaddling was abandoned in the later eighteenth and early nineteenth centuries, the lack of necessity for knobs affected the design of cradles.

In the 1740s a number of essays and pamphlets were published, in English and not Latin, on child-rearing. Dr William Cadogan was just one physician who attacked the practice of swaddling and he recommended that infants should have their limbs left unhindered by bindings. During the eighteenth century swaddling became out of favour among the upper classes in Europe, and in the following century cotton, linen, flannel and then woollen binders came into use instead. These were placed around the stomach of the baby, initially to support the dressing for the umbilical cord. By the 1920s a narrow roll of flannel or wool, considered essential as infant underwear, was the only relic of swaddling clothes.

Interestingly enough, some 'baby' doctors today have realized that newborn infants become calm when swaddled.

*Medieval babies were tightly swaddled with bands in a criss-cross fashion*

# Cots, Cradles and Cribs

ONCE an infant's hunger is satisfied its most pressing need then is often for sleep. In the Bible, Mary was forced to place her baby son in a stable manger which served as his crib, having no other alternative. Every baby must have a crib of some kind, even if that is nothing more than a basket made out of branches and filled with moss, or a deep drawer in a bedroom dresser, in order that he or she can be supported while mother is getting some well-earned rest.

The idea of a special bed in which to lay a baby undoubtedly is an ancient one. Greeks and Romans seemed to have used stools on wheels which could be rolled backwards and forwards, having much the same effect as a rocking cradle in soothing a baby. The most primitive tribes constructed basin-like objects in which to place their infants while the parents were busy doing other things. Often the cradles were suspended from the ceiling of a hut, ideally located so that the mother could give the cradle a gentle push as she passed and lull the baby to sleep.

We know, also, that infants were placed in baskets – which have become known to us as 'Moses' baskets, wooden trough-like objects and even saucer-shaped ceramic pots. Some of the earliest cradles were hollowed-out tree boughs which were set on the ground. But few infant items have survived. Many cradles and cribs were discarded once they were no longer useful and, if they were made of wood – which presents itself as the most obvious material – they were most likely broken up and used for firewood.

The development of the cradle (being an infant bed with some sort of rocking motion, often a simple wooden box with extended rockers for

pushing), the crib (a small rectangular bed which is stationary and free-standing) and the cot (which is stationary but larger and has high sides) came much more recently in our history. Many scholars offer the opinion that the fact that there were cradles in the Middle Ages was due to the work of priests who created nativity scenes in their churches complete with the baby Jesus in a manger. They suggest that people who came to see the nativity scene went home and built cribs for their children. However, it would be short-sighted to assume that even the most makeshift cradles, made out of scraps of wood, were non-existent prior to that time.

Certainly, cradles appeared in medieval manuscripts. At a time when beds were scarce and privacy was something that only the exceptionally wealthy could afford, if, indeed, they desired it, most medieval homes did not have a special piece of furniture for a child. Beds were expensive to produce, costing far more than anyone but a lord could afford. The wealthy travelled with their own beds, otherwise they would be required to share with strangers or bed down in the straw with everyone else. Infants slept with their siblings or parents.

For the well-to-do, cradles in medieval times were made of oak, which was often carved with flowers, leaves and the baby's initials and the year of its birth. These sturdy objects were at first built low to the ground but over the centuries they were made taller so that mother did not have to bend so far. They had canopies to protect the babies from draughts in uninsulated homes and the coverlets and hangings mimicked those of medieval beds.

As a cradle was seen as a status symbol, the wealthier the parents, the richer the hangings. Silk, prized treasure of the East, found its way to the European markets through Genoa or Venice, then through France. Nothing was too good for an important baby, the heir to a throne or inheritor of a vast estate. There was velvet to wrap a child in and fur with which to line the cradle, trim robes and make coverlets. Carefully worked quilts, undoubtedly something the mother would have occupied herself with during her pregnancy, were used also to keep the infant warm. It was not unknown for babies, wrapped in swaddling clothes and covered with heavy silks, velvets and furs, to suffocate.

Lollay, lollay, little child, the fote is in the whele:
Thou nost whoder turned, to wo other wele.

[*Lollay, lollay, little child, your foot is on Fortune's wheel, and you do not know which way it will turn, to pain or prosperity.*]

Fourteenth-century lullaby

*A seventeenth-century carved wood cradle decorated with acanthus leaves. It has a deep hood to protect the occupant from draughts and the knobs were used for tying the child inside or for winding wool*

95

ROCK-A-BYE BABY
Rock–a–bye baby, on the tree
    top,
When the wind blows the cradle
    will rock;
when the bough breaks the
    cradle will fall,
and down will come baby, cradle
    and all.

*Not surprisingly few seventeenth- and eighteenth-century wickerwork cradles survive today. Lightweight, they were easy to transport and many were taken to the USA from Europe*

For the less well-to-do, crib coverings were still most important. The poorest people would cover the baby in old garments which had been cut down to size to fit around the crib; others who could knit, sew or weave took great pride in making coverlets and blankets for their offspring. Paintings from the nineteenth century, which depict an extraordinarily large number of babies, usually show babies almost smothered in layer upon layer of cotton and wool.

Sixteenth-century physicians recommended putting infants in cradles except immediately after feeding when they felt that the infant was likely to be sick. Swinging cots, higher off the ground and supported between two rigid posts, became popular. Very few cradles exist from this century but by this time caning, marquetry and veneering were known so it is likely that cradles and cribs were made which employed these methods of decoration. Barley-twist legs were used on other pieces of furniture, so why not cradles?

One kind of cradle which survives today from the seventeenth century was made of panelled oak, with a wooden headboard, or a hood which was often hinged, and knobs which were used to tie the baby in with the bindings of his swaddling clothes, or for the mother to wind wool around while she rocked the cradle with her feet. At first rockers were pinned to the cradle through the end posts of the body of the cradle, but later they were attached to the bottom of the cradle.

A number of seventeenth-century cots were made of wicker, also having deep canopies, but they have not survived in any great numbers. Walnut replaced oak at this time, but walnut was ultimately replaced by mahogany, then satinwood and, by the late nineteenth century, by rosewood.

Other seventeenth-century cradles were designed to swing between two uprights, and these became known, confusingly, as 'cots', until the early twentieth century. Some of the early cradles were quite large as children of two or three years of age would be expected to sleep in them, unless a younger brother or sister usurped them. In many ways things have changed very little. Today we put infants in large cots in which we expect them to sleep until they are old enough for their own beds.

In the eighteenth century lavish marquetry examples were made with a great deal of ornamentation. These cradles were dressed in silk and satin, and lined with fur, and plumes and feathers decorated the top

of the canopy. Some cradles even had gilded handles for the 'rocker', the person entrusted to rock the child, who would have been specifically employed for this purpose in wealthy households. In poorer homes the youngest child would be assigned this task.

It was during the eighteenth century that slatted and spindled cradles first became popular. These cradles became fashionable as a result of contemporary writers who felt that fresh air was good for babies, rather than the claustrophobia of closed-in cradles and too many coverings. Cribs and cradles with caned sides, often supported by the new wood, mahogany, were made from about 1720, alongside the suspended swinging cradle which endured throughout the century.

But it was the nineteenth century when infant furniture really came into its own. This was due largely, of course, to the fact that many Victorian homes had a special room in which to put infants with their own scaled-down furniture – the nursery. Along with the nursery came nanny and an extraordinary number of new ideas on raising children. The idea that rocking was unsuitable for babies had started at the end of the eighteenth century and by the first half of the nineteenth century rocking cradles were denounced as being the cause of brain damage and a long list of other dreadful ailments. Stationary, raised cribs became permanent fixtures in Victorian homes. They were passed down from one generation to the next. Queen Victoria's children all slept in turn in the same carved wooden cradle and wore the same christening robe. Sir Edwin Landseer painted Princess Alice asleep in the cradle, a commissioned birthday gift from Prince Albert to the Queen.

As writers on child-care proliferated, Victorians turned their attentions to babies. They concerned themselves not only with how and where babies slept, but also with the design of cradles and cots, and they debated whether the hood should be made of leather, wood or wicker. New technology and the fresh-air fad with which we have come to identify the whole century resulted in the permanent adoption of slatted and spindled cribs, from which we have inherited the children's cots of today and the disappearance of the heavy, carved, wooden cradle.

*This dainty cot trimmed with muslin lace and wide satin ribbon bows was available from the Army & Navy stores in 1907 for £3. 17s. 6d.*

97

The health obsession also produced iron cribs with so-called 'hygienic' mattresses, some made of rubber, which came into use in the nineteenth century.

Cradles, cots and cribs were shown at the Great Exhibition in 1851 and playpens and baby walkers were advertised in magazines. Some mothers, convinced that baby needed as much fresh air as possible, suspended their offspring on a tray-like apparatus outside the nursery window. The fashion for fresh air in the 1840s heralded the way for the arrival of the perambulator.

The 'berceaunette', or bassinet as it became known, was a basin-shaped cradle usually raised on legs, often made of wicker, which was curtained to the ground. this was a popular item in the USA where today cribs are called bassinets. Another particularly American cradle was the low-to-the-ground cradle found in the homes of early settlers. Some adult versions of these cradles exist, presumably for those who needed the rhythmic motion to soothe them.

*A German eighteenth-century iron cot with an adjustable hood*

### A CRADLE SONG

Sweet dreams, form a shade
O'er my lovely infant's head;
Sweet dreams of pleasant streams
By happy, silent, moony beams.

Sweet sleep, with soft down
Weave thy brows an infant crown
Sweet sleep, Angel mild,
Hover o'er my happy child.

Sweet smiles, in the night
Hover over my delight;
Sweet smiles, Mother's smiles,
All the livelong night beguiles.

Sweet moans, dovelike sighs,
Chase not slumber from thy eyes.
Sweet moans, sweeter smiles,
All the dovelike moans beguiles.

Sleep, sleep, happy child,
All creation slept and smil'd;
Sleep, sleep, happy sleep;
While o'er thee thy mother weep.

Sweet babe, in thy face
Holy image I can trace.
Sweet babe, once like thee,
Thy maker lay and wept for me.

Wept for me, for thee, for all,
When he was an infant small.
Thou his image ever see,
Heavenly face that smiles on thee,

Smiles on thee, on me, on all;
Who became an infant small.
Infant smiles are his own smiles;
Heaven and earth to peace beguiles.

William Blake

## COTS, CRADLES AND CRIBS

American Indians created a unique kind of cradle which we call a cradle board. It is made of an elliptical frame which has wooden lathes laid across it, and a board at the baby's feet which can be lowered as the baby grows. The child is laced inside with buckskin which also forms a hood around the cradle board.

By the turn of the century the heavy wooden cradles of earlier years had been replaced by a new folding cot which was well suited to the smaller homes of the twentieth century. Cot sheets, pillow cases, eiderdowns and

*An Arts and Crafts cradle designed in 1867 by Norman Shaw*

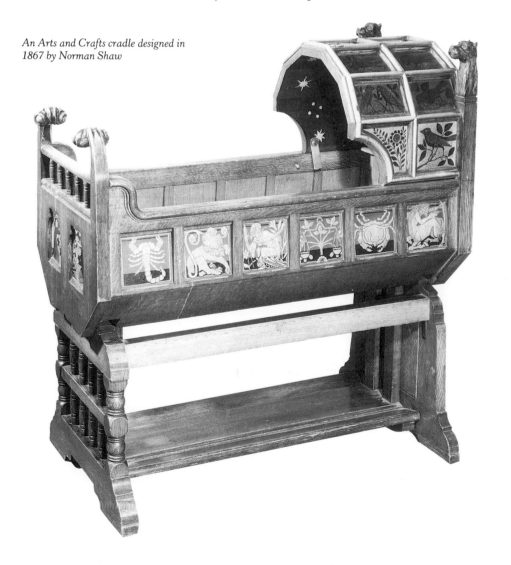

## GOLDEN SLUMBERS

Golden slumbers kiss your eyes,
Smiles awake you when you rise.
Sleep, pretty wantons, do not
    cry,
    And I will sing a lullaby:
Rock them, rock them, lullaby.

Care is heavy, therefore sleep
    you:
You are care, and care must keep
    you.
Sleep, pretty wantons, do not
    cry,
    And I will sing a lullaby:
Rock them, rock them, lullaby.

                Thomas Dekker

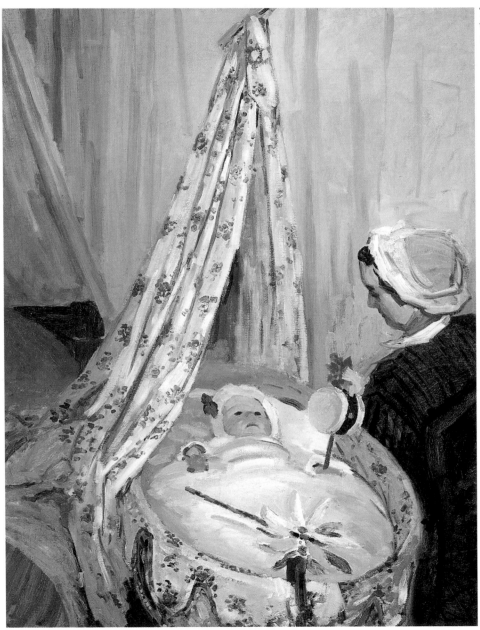

The Cradle – Camille with
the Artist's Son *Jean by
Claude Monet, 1867*

100

coverlets were all readily available from stores, which also sold elaborate trimmings. The twentieth-century mother could have her choice of plain or fancy. When her child got a little older she could put him in a child's crib, described by the manufacturers as a piece of equipment 'no family, rich or poor, should be without. A patent common-sense folding child's crib' which formed an extension to mother's own bed. It was advertised as 'Cheap. Ornamental. Useful and healthful.'

The twentieth century saw the arrival of the carry cot, a rectangular lightweight cot with handles on either side for carrying, which could be secured on to a pram base. When not in use as a pram the carry cot could be brought indoors and used as a floor cot.

Lullabies (from the word 'lullay', which was sung) existed long before there were cradles in which to rock babies. Early lullabies, dating from the twelfth and thirteenth centuries and no longer in use, were popular songs of the day which were more often than not bawdy in content. No one thought anything of singing them to an infant who couldn't understand the words anyway. Nurses, minders and 'rockers' generally were not sufficiently well educated to know more genteel verses, but despite this there were songs, crooned and sung, especially for babies.

In French the word for a lullaby is *berceuse*, and its relation to the nineteenth-century cot is obvious. Perhaps some of the most famous lullabies were written by composers, Schumann, Chopin and Brahms, and popular words are still sung to at least one of these today. It is really within the last one hundred and fifty years that most children's literature, and cradle songs, were written, although *Mother Goose's Melody: or Sonnets for the Cradle* was published in London in 1781 by the firm of John Newbery, and four years later in the USA by Isaiah Thomas. It included such favourites as 'Jack and Jill', 'Ding Dong Bell', and 'Hush-a-Bye Baby on the Tree Top'.

*From left to right:*

*Cradle cots, as these were called, were made of iron. They were popular in the early twentieth century when houses were smaller and cot manufacturers responded by producing portable folding cots*

*An early American cradle. Many were made of pine but painted to resemble mahogany*

*This folding cradle from 1916 belonged to a baby who died only a few days old. The cradle and layette were never used again*

ON THE DEATH OF A
CHILD

The greatest griefs shall find
  themselves inside the
  smallest cage.
It's only then that we can
  hope to tame their rage,

The monsters we must live
  with. For it will not do
To hiss humanity because
  one human threw
Us out of heart and home.
  Or part

At odds with life because
  one baby failed to live.
Indeed, as little as its subject,
  is the wreath we give –

The big words fail to fit. Like
  giant boxes
Round small bodies. Taking
  up improper room,
Where so much withering is,
  and so much bloom.

D. J. Enright

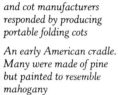

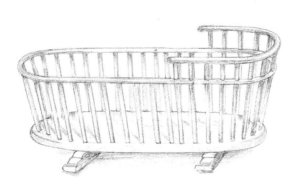

# The Arcutio

Privacy is a relatively modern concept. In the past, most houses had few rooms and those rooms were shared by many people. Master, mistress and servants were known to bed down in the same room. When houses became larger, with more rooms, and when beds were more readily available and affordable, people still slept together. Wealthy people travelled with their own beds so that they would not be obliged to share with strangers at an inn, where they broke their journey for the night.

Babies were no exception. Cribs and cradles were used only by the very rich and a newborn baby would be bundled into bed with its parents and/or brothers or sisters. Many infants died by being smothered by one or two people with whom they shared a bed. 'Overlaying', as it was called, was often cited as a reason for the death of a child in parish workhouse registers. Drunken nurses were usually named as the culprits.

In Italy this problem was solved by placing the child in an arcutio. This was a wooden contraption, measuring a little over three foot in length wider at the head than the feet, into which the child was placed. Each side had deep grooves to enable the child to breast-feed when necessary during the night and a bar supported the nurse, preventing her from falling on her charge.

## The ARCUTIO.

*This strange-looking contraption was in use in Italy in the seventeenth century recommended for a child that could be 'safely laid entirely under the Bed Cloaths in the Winter, without Danger or smothering'*

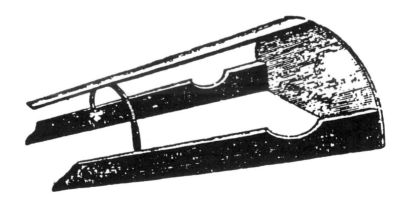

# THE MIDWIFE'S TALE
## NORTHERN ENGLAND, IN THE MID 1780s

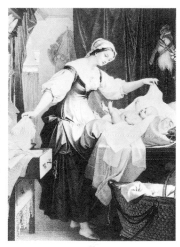

She was almost asleep when the child banged on the door. It took her some time to get up off the floor, her legs being what they were, old and worn and tired of traipsing through the dark, all weathers. One birth after another – they all seemed to come in the small hours.

The child was kicking at the door by the time she got there. A small grubby face, one she didn't recognize.

'It's me Mam,' he said, wide-eyed. 'Baby's gon stuck.'

The old woman sighed.

'Who's yer Mam?'

'Out at farm.' The boy jerked his head. 'Me Dad said for you to come.'

The midwife turned back into her cottage. She was already wearing her boots but she pulled an old woollen frock over her shift and settled two shawls about her shoulders. It was cold out there and she'd have to walk over the hill to the farm. No telling how long it would take in the dark. She hoped the child knew his way.

Her one-room abode had a makeshift closet in the far corner. She shuffled over and withdrew a basket, over which she placed a cloth. As she closed the door of her cottage behind her she knew the sun would be up before she would see home again.

It was a pity, she thought, as the boy led the way into the night, that they didn't know more up at the farm about birthing babies. You'd think that they'd have learned something from all the cows and sheep but no, they always called her, often when it was too late for her to do anything other than tell them to fetch the man-midwife with his hooks and knives. A real shame, that's what it was. People would sooner have a man doing women's business. What did he know? Just because he spent all day cutting up sheep, it didn't mean he knew anything about women and babies. Still, she had to work alongside him plenty of times.

Owls hooted their way through the wood. Once or twice the old woman stumbled over things she couldn't see. She reached out to hold on to the boy's smock. It was thin worn fabric, and she was frightened she might tear it. Half-way up the hill she took off one of her shawls and wound it around the boy's shoulders.

She didn't know this family. They must be the new sheep-herder's family she'd heard the farm-manager's wife speak of when she was last at the farm. She'd been delivering babies at the farm for years now, just like her mother used to do before her. This farm-manager's wife was a strong woman. Just as well, considering that her husband seemed bent on giving her a new child just as soon as she'd got one weaned. The midwife had delivered nine of her children so far and only two had died. The farm-manager always gave her more eggs if his wife had a boy. As if it was anything to do with her!

They climbed up the steep hill and on top she stopped to catch her breath. In the clearing below, by the sliver of light from the moon, she could make out the farmhouse.

Once, when she came to the farm, they put her in a cart and drove her to York. It took all day, and the farm-manager drove her himself, agitated all the while that the woman would have the baby before they got there. She'd asked him if they didn't have midwives in York but he'd pretended not to hear. She'd never been to York before and would have liked to stay longer but she didn't have any say in the matter.

It turned out that the woman in labour was the wife of the man who owned the farm and all the land about it. He might as well have been the king for all the midwife knew; she'd never set foot off his land before in her life. His wife had never carried a baby to term before and the landowner, wanting the best for his wife, had applied to the farm-manager for the name of a midwife. And now the woman wouldn't let the midwife examine her. 'It's all the same to me,' the old woman told her. 'Women are all the same under their skirts. You don't have anything different than what I have.' Except you've got a baby in there, she thought, and some-

how I've got to get it out of you.

The boy beside pulled on her shawl. Holding on to each other's shoulders together they half-walked, half-slid in a muddy path down the hill. She was glad of her boots.

By the light from the fire in the hearth, and the few flickering candles, she recognized the boy's mother, though she'd not delivered her before. The woman could barely speak, she was so exhausted. She lay on a raised straw pallet on one side of the room. The midwife approached, shooing away the children, three, maybe four, of them. They scuttled off past her feet, into the dark corners. She set her basket down.

'Which one of you's the eldest?' she asked in the direction of the corner.

The boy who had brought her here stepped up.

'Well, you. Go unlock all the doors and windows in the house. There's nothing to be left locked, understand? That'll help bring the baby out. Where's your sister?'

A girl of about six came out of the shadows.

'Go find yer Mam's stitching and unpick it, all of it, quick now! That baby inside can't take up any more of your Mam's time!'

She turned to the father who sat in a chair in the corner, hopeless and helpless, though he'd been through this Lord knows how many times before.

'I'll need a pot of hot water. A piece of coal. Some salt. One of your old smocks. How long's she been like this?'

The man shrugged.

'She was like it when I come 'ome.'

The midwife bent over the woman and felt her abdomen. Muttering under her breath she made her examination. In the background a wail told her that there was a youngster waiting to be fed. She shook her head.

'The baby's twisted around,' she told the woman. 'I don't know as I can help you.'

'Oh, please,' the woman gasped between spasms of pain. 'He wanted to send for the man-midwife but he'll kill me, or my baby. I heard about you. You delivered good babies for the farm-manager's wife. Help me!'

The midwife took off her shawl and pushed the sleeves of her frock over her elbows. She'd done this once before, turned a baby, but she was younger then and she'd been with the woman from the first, not like this, called in last thing.

It was almost dawn before her efforts proved successful. One of the other women from the farm came in to help. The father, having set a pot of water over the fire, left for work. She didn't know where the children had got to but someone must have fed the baby as it had stopped crying.

As the first fingers of sunlight came through the clouds the woman gave birth to a scrawny boy. The old woman stuck her finger in his mouth and wiped his eyes. She fished for her scissors in her basket and cut the umbilical cord, tying a scrap of fabric around the baby's middle over his navel. She spat on his forehead to keep the Evil Eye at bay and rubbed him all over with salt before washing him in the water heating over the fire. Some women she knew liked to plunge the newborn's feet into cold water to toughen them up, but she'd never liked that idea. She was not fond of cold water herself, especially not on the feet, and couldn't see that it would help the baby much.

The other woman helped the mother. The afterbirth was scooped up in the straw and one of the children, who seemed to have emerged from nowhere to see his new brother, was sent running for a bucket. On her bed, the mother called out for something to drink. Her daughter fetched a jug of ale and the woman took a deep draught.

The midwife sent another child for the baby's pap spoon, but before she fed the newborn she took a cup and swilled it in the water over the fire. Then she measured out some water, picked up the piece of coal, which the father had set nearby her, and dropped it into the cup. This was 'cinder tea' which she gave the baby to keep the devil away, putting her fingers first in the cup, then in the baby's mouth.

Then she gave it a spoonful of pap to clean out all the excrement that had built up during the months inside its mother. The old woman wasn't really sure if it worked but that was what people did then and she didn't want to run the risk of anything going wrong.

When the girls had finished tearing

up their father's shirt they handed the pieces to her so that she could swaddle the baby. Swaddling took a long time, and she liked to do it right. The poor little thing might as well be comfortable; it could be several days before the swaddling bands were changed. She took the biggest piece and laid it under the boy, wrapping either end across his limbs, then bringing the lower piece up between his legs and folding it across his stomach. The other pieces she wrapped around and around him, even his head, until he was a smooth padded bundle. Now he would grow tall and strong, all his limbs having been set in their proper place.

The two girls watched her carefully. Their mother, who hadn't yet seen the child, fell back asleep on the straw. When the midwife finished, the eldest girl reached for the infant.

'Put him down next to his Mam,' the midwife told her. 'Don't take him outside, the fairies might get him. You keep an eye on both of them, now.'

The midwife began collecting her things together. The eldest boy came in and she sent him out again with instructions to dig a hole in the earth, not far from the cottage. The midwife carried the pail containing the afterbirth outside. They buried it with the straw and the boy covered up the hole with mud.

She walked part of the way back home with the other woman. They said it was a pity the father hadn't stayed. They would have liked something to eat and drink themselves. It wasn't every day a man got a son, and a healthy one at that. No doubt the man would be around in a few days to give her a handful of coins, grunting his thanks. If the child died, she might not see him at all, but she could expect a few things from the mother, delivered to her door by one of the children. Those children would get to know her. If she lived much longer she'd probably be called upon to deliver that eldest girl. That was how things happened around this part of the country.

Lullaby and goodnight,
Let angels of light
Spread wings round your bed
And guard you from dread.
When the lark leaves his nest
God will wake you from rest,
When the lark leaves his nest
God will wake you from rest.

Johannes Brahms

# NEW BABY

# As Well As Can Be Expected

*This sixteenth-century Swiss woodcut of a lying-in room shows mother being offered sustenance after the birth of her child, who is being washed. Another child plays near the cradle with a doll, a wooden 'poppet'. On the table lie the midwife's tools*

S O many aspects of birth are ritualistic, both for the baby and the mother, and the presence of other women in the birthing room, midwives, 'gossips', friends and families – until the man-midwife chased them out – fulfilled a number of functions. Several women would be present for the sole purpose of supporting the mother during the birth and securing her comfort afterwards when the midwife was busy with the new baby. Others, particularly younger women, were there to learn and to witness an aspect of womanhood they might previously know little or nothing about.

In most cultures it is customary to wash the baby immediately after the birth. Hard soaps were not available until the twelfth century but even after that date most midwives washed babies with herbal concoctions and water. The tradition in the eighteenth century was to wash the baby and then scour it with salt. The new baby would have been purged of the excrement which was believed to have been built up inside it during the months in the womb by being given an emetic of syrup of roses, oil of almonds, castor oil or anything else the midwife had handy such as wine, whisky, oatmeal, caudle or panada.

In parts of England, a newborn's head was washed in rum for luck. In other places babies were given cinder tea, boiled water in which a piece of coal had been dropped or water in which the sap from the ash tree had been mixed. It was common all over Europe to give the infant a dab of butter and a little sugar to signify the hoped-for riches that the child would have in the future.

The caul, which sometimes covered the head of an infant, was highly treasured and credited with magical powers. A caul was bequeathed to

110

members of the same family, as the idea accompanying the caul was that if it left the family there would be a loss of power and subsequent grief. Many people thought that the caul prevented death by drowning.

In most aspects of birth, royal children received different treatment from the general populace. The birth of a royal child would be an occasion for national celebration. In France cannons were sounded in the street and free wine was distributed amongst the people. The baby who would grow up to be Louis XIV was powdered with a mixture of myrrh, cumin, crushed calves' feet and powdered snails' shells. He was washed in oil of roses and red wine before being swaddled in fine linen and placed in elaborately embroidered blankets with a lace cap on his head. His swaddling clothes were changed several times a day.

Curiously enough, there are a number of rites which take place concerning the afterbirth and the umbilical cord. Many people associated the length of the cut umbilical cord with the length that a male child's penis would grow. In primitive tribes the cord is cut and then washed and wiped dry with grass before being buried. One African tribe keeps the umbilical cord wrapped in a piece of cloth which is then hung to a post. The cord from a male is used to treat ailments of young girls while the cord from a girl is used to treat illnesses in boys. The cord is often seen as a symbol of strength and health in the child, and it is hung up in the home as a talisman. Some peoples of the Philippines will not cut the umbilical cord until the placenta has been completely expelled. If it is the first birth, a tiny piece of placenta is charred, pulverized and mixed with water, which is then given to the mother to drink.

Placentas were often buried, and special burial jars, dating back to the fifteenth and sixteenth centuries, have been discovered in Korea. In fourteenth-century Europe the placenta and umbilical cord were tied to a fruit-bearing tree. The afterbirth was buried under trees and shrubs, or flung out to sea. Sometimes ritualistic songs were sung or chanted, and grandmothers and older women were present to make sure that all the procedures were carried out correctly so that the child would lead a long and happy life.

In most cultures the exhausted mother was washed and dressed by her female helpers. She would be given something to drink: ale, wine and later, when it became drinkable, water, broth or caudle, the latter being made of a mix of oatmeal, gruel, raisins, spices, rum or Madeira, which was designed to build up her strength.

The old, bad days, when every woman was supposed to know by instinct how to nurse, feed and teach children have gone forever; the art of looking after children is *recognized* as an art — if not a science.

*The Nursery World*, Wednesday, 2 December 1925, first issue

Although some women, especially those of American Indian tribes, felt strong enough to go back to work immediately after the birth of their child, most felt the need for rest. Even if they wished to get back on their feet shortly after giving birth, until fairly recently society prevented them from doing so.

Giving birth was considered in the past to be unclean. Ancient Greeks smeared pitch on the door of the house where a woman was in labour to warn others to stay away. In tribal villages all over the world, birthing huts are still constructed today, some distance away from the rest of the huts, where women are sent when they are ready to deliver. Many women remain in these huts for up to one month after the birth.

In European and American societies, until the second half of this century, the birthing process – both labour and the post-partum period – was called the 'lying-in'. While it was generally reserved for the middle and upper classes who did not work, and who could afford a 'monthly' nurse to take over the running of the household, the rules of isolation still applied because all women had to be 'churched' before they were allowed to re-enter society. The monthly nurse was generally an older woman who was often present before the birth and was expected to deliver the baby in the absence of the midwife or doctor. Less is known about her in history than other female figures, but it it safe to assume that good monthly nurses, rather like good midwives, were passed around the family and from one woman to another. The notorious Mrs Gamp was a self-described monthly nurse.

In the past women were expected to remain in bed much longer than they are today. It would be unthinkable for a woman in the nineteenth century to book herself into hospital for a few hours in order to give birth, as one can do today. Women in the early part of this century were encouraged to stay in bed for at least a week, with the curtains drawn, the room heated and sheltered from any draughts. Fresh air was considered to be most unhealthy; although medical writers in the 1700s believed fresh air to be beneficial, it was the late 1800s before the idea was widely adopted.

In the nineteenth century, once the new mother had removed herself from her bed she would pass the day in her dressing room, reclining on a couch. Dressed in the loose robes of her maternity, or special nursing dresses with slanted pockets on both breasts so that she could feed the baby without completely undressing, the new mother would receive intimate female friends and close female relatives.

*A more modern style of painting in the early twentieth century admitted greater intimacy as in Frederick William Elwell's work* The First Born *painted in 1913*

The second week she would receive visits from other family members and acquaintances, while during the third and fourth weeks, when she may well have descended to the parlour, she would receive male relatives and anyone else who was curious to see the baby. The ritual of birth extended to the visitors. Female friends and relatives visiting a mother and newborn baby would put on their best clothes and carry gifts to the pair. Close family members made pin cushions with the words 'Welcome Sweet Baby', or 'Welcome Little Stranger', worked into the fabric. Many parents saw their new baby as just that: a miniature person, a stranger whom they called 'it'. Blankets, cot covers, clothing, rattles and bells were brought to the new baby, just as they are today. Visitors would be given a cup of caudle to drink and the baby, who was dressed up for the occasion, would be brought downstairs in his or her crib to be admired by the party.

113

HUSH, LITTLE BABY

Hush little baby don't say a
  word,
Mama's gonna buy you a
  mockin' bird.

If that mockin' bird don't sing,
Papa's gonna buy you a diamond
  ring.

If that ring is made of brass,
Mama's gonna buy you a lookin'
  glass.

If that lookin' glass gets broke,
Papa's gonna buy you a billy
  goat.

If that billy goat don't pull,
Mama's gonna buy you a cart
  and bull.

If that cart and bull turn over,
Papa's gonna buy you a dog
  named Rover.

If that dog named Rover don't
  bark,
Mama's gonna buy you a horse
  and cart.

If that horse and cart fall down,
You'll be the sweetest little boy
  in town!

In Ancient Rome an olive branch would be hung from the front door of a house when a boy was born, and a strip of woollen fabric if the child was a girl. Eighteenth-century London homes hung strips of ribbon on their door knockers, pink for a girl and blue for a boy. When the present Prince Charles was born the fountains in Trafalgar Square ran blue. Even until fairly recently villagers in Northumberland gave a cheese to the men in local households if a boy was born, but to the women for a girl.

Although no one quite knows why, it was thought to be bad luck in some parts of the country to have a baby in the month of May, and May babies were considered sickly. Even animals born in the month of May were thought to be particularly troublesome. Sunday was viewed as the luckiest day of the week on which to have a child and Christmas Day the luckiest day of the year. On the other hand 28 December, Childermas, was thought to be the unluckiest day for a woman to give birth, which was probably connected with the fact that 28 December is the day of Holy Innocents when, according to the Bible, Herod ordered all the infants to be slain. The famous rhyme tells us which days of the week were thought to be favourable:

Monday's child is fair of face,
Tuesday's child is full of grace,
Wednesday's child is full of woe,
Thursday's child has far to go,
Friday's child is loving and giving,
Saturday's child works hard for a living,
But the child that is born on the Sabbath day
Is bonny and blithe and good and gay.

The earlier in the day that a child was born the better, and the child born during the waxing moon was thought to grow very quickly. A 'chime child' was one born between midnight on Friday and cockcrow on Saturday, although in different parts of the world a chime child can be one born at four, eight or twelve o'clock or at three, six, nine or twelve o'clock. Chime children are supposed to have second sight.

For many women, and this is still true today in many parts of the world, the birth of a child would make her the focus of attention only for the second time in her life, the first time being on her wedding day. In aristocratic households, the wife who produced the family heir very often received a

A Visit to the Young Mother. *When it was time to go downstairs mother and baby received visits from female friends and relatives. Painted by Jean Carolus in 1871*

financial reward, or a gift of jewellery from her husband. It was at this point that mother-in-laws often took it upon themselves to remind their son-in-laws, as discreetly as possible, to leave their wives alone. Madame de Sévigné's letters of the seventeenth century to her daughter and son-in-law, the Count and Countess de Grignan, contain suggestions that the Count should leave his wife alone once she had fulfilled her duties and provided him with an heir. Madame de Sévigné's biographers suggest that the Grignans objected to her interference, and in any event her suggestion did nothing to alter the situation: the Countess de Grignan had seven pregnancies in as many years, by which time her husband had given her syphilis.

Eighteenth-century women were confined to the house for a period of four to six weeks after the birth. This period became increasingly shorter during the nineteenth century when doctors began to understand, and treat, childbed fever. One of the greatest causes of death to women in childbirth prior to this

time was due to the infections received at the unhygienic hands of medical practitioners and midwives, and the unsterile conditions in hospitals. In the twentieth century, once medicine had identified the sources of the disease and had the means, in the form of antibiotics, to fight it, childbed fever (puerperal sepsis) became a rarity. From a social point of view, women were not encouraged to leave the house until the 'churching' of the mother took place, which was usually followed by the christening of the child. The former ceremony existed in ancient times. Hebrew law specified that a woman was not able to enter a holy place for thirty-three days after giving birth to a boy, and sixty-six days after giving birth to a girl. As childbirth has been considered 'unclean' for centuries, the idea was to keep the new mother away from the rest of the population. In some societies women were not allowed to make food for their families until they had been churched. Only when she was properly cleansed by a local religious figure was it permissible for her to rejoin the congregation.

Over the centuries the idea of churching the woman became firmly associated with cleansing her, but in fact the service is one of thanksgiving for a safe delivery and recovery for the mother, and four to six weeks was considered to be a period of time when the mother was out of danger of childbed-related diseases. Many women put great emphasis on this ceremony, grateful to have the opportunity to give thanks and be seen back in the community. Wealthy women even had special dresses made for the event.

Other than the lying-in, and the subsequent churching of the mother, very little thought was given to her physical or emotional welfare. Deformed children were thought to be the responsibility of the mother for thinking evil thoughts during her pregnancy, and post-natal depression was not acknowledged by the medical profession until the 1920s: although it had been noted by early writers on childbirth it had not been explained.

Once the mother had been churched and the christening had taken place, if the less well-off mother had not gone back to work already, now she would do so. Wealthy women would turn over the raising of their children to the servants in the nursery upstairs where nurses, nannies and governesses would take over until the children were sent away to school.

*The Model Family by Eva Hollyer (fl. 1891–98)*

116

AS WELL AS CAN BE EXPECTED

# Twins

'Two for the price of one' is the saying most often heard at the birth of twins. People in the past have found nothing more puzzling than twins and even today, when we understand how twins and other multiple births are created, these babies, especially identical sets, often make headline news. So-called identical twins, resulting from the split of a single fertilized egg after conception, have the same chromosomes but despite appearances they are never exactly identical. Fraternal twins are created from two fertilized eggs and they are not necessarily alike.

The average 'twin' pregnancy is shorter than a normal pregnancy. Labour also tends to be shorter and in the past, as with anything that was out of the ordinary, this was viewed with fear, and witchcraft was suspected. It was also impossible until fairly recently to diagnose twins, and the surprise of a plural birth, to both mother and doctor, only served to fuel suspicious minds.

Around the world people fall roughly into two groups concerning twins: those who desire twins and honour them within their cultures and those who view them with fear and dread. Happily, the latter group now consists mainly of a few primitive tribes whose understanding of conception is less than rudimentary. There are numerous explanations, many of them greatly amusing, as to why twins are born. People often felt that it was the mother's fault, that her thoughts had created two children, or that she was over-sexed. In the Middle Ages, there were stories of mothers who gave birth to rabbits and twin monsters, brought about, so people believed, by the mother's thoughts during pregnancy. One African tribe, the Kaffirs, punished the mother of twins as an adulteress as twins were thought to have been created by two different fathers.

A common belief around the world was that twins could be created if a pregnant woman ate fruit that was 'twinned', such as bananas, or any fruit that had to be split in some way before it could be eaten.

In Tanganyika, Africa, certain tribes believe that the dead below the ground produced twins and pregnant women were advised to stay close to the house and avoid meeting people in case they came into contact in some way with spirits of the dead. Once born, twins were mourned and two huts were built, one for the mother and twins, one for the father. In the village women

cooked food for the family and brought it to them for about a month until the family, and the whole village including the animals, were anointed in a purification ceremony designed to prevent further births of twins.

The Nootka Indians of Vancouver Island actively encouraged the birth of twins by ritually bathing in a lake. They believed that twins came from another world and that they were relatives of the Salmon spirits which lived under the sea. Twins were regarded with a great deal of respect and they were believed to have healing powers. Other peoples credit twins with having powers of clairvoyancy.

Unfortunately, the ignorance surrounding the birth of twins in the past has resulted in infanticide. The Apache Indians ritually killed one twin, arguing that the mother did not have sufficient milk to feed two infants, and some Eskimo people left one twin outside to die in the cold.

In some parts of the world there is an unconscious belief that twins are in fact one person, and accordingly they are dressed alike and treated in the same manner. Specialists now do not encourage this behaviour and stress, particularly to the mother of identical twins, that each child should be treated individually. Today, the other most-often-heard saying about twins is 'twice the fun, twice the work'.

# Wetting the Baby's Head

T HE toast we drink to the new baby and mother is not just an excuse to celebrate with a glass of champagne. 'Wetting the baby's head', as we call it, has a very deep-rooted symbolism attached to it. With the spread of Christian doctrine in the Western world came the belief that immersion in water washed away sins. As birth was viewed as the result of sin, it was important that an infant be washed of any taint of childbirth.

In almost every culture there is some sort of ceremony which has the purpose of formally admitting the child into the religious and/or social world. Until this time the child is viewed, even today, as being unwholesome in some way. Just as women were required to go through a 'churching', the baptism and accompanying christening or naming of a child gave it a new start, with a new name, free from the unhealthy associations of childbirth.

An unbaptized infant was not entitled to a proper burial, but buried in a corner of the churchyard with nameless vagrants and people who had committed suicide. As many newborn infants did not reach childhood, early baptisms were necessary in the past.

For centuries the baptism of infants involved ducking the child, his legs and arms held by his godparents, under flowing water or into a font. King Ethelred, born around AD 968, was supposed to have taken this moment to urinate in his font. If the child screamed during the baptism service, which was more than likely after it had been stripped of its clothing in a cold church then ducked in equally cold water, it was seen as a good sign, indicating that the child itself was chasing the devil away.

120

Godparents are believed by some scholars to have evolved from 'gossips', the labour-room companions of the expectant mother, but this does not explain male godparents. With the high incidence of death in childbirth, it was sensible to appoint people who were both willing and able to provide for the child, as advisers on spiritual matters as well as providers of financial support, in the absence of one or both parents. Traditional godparents, who were two of the baby's sex and one of the other, vowed to keep the child from water, fire, horse's foot and hound's tooth for seven years.

In time, the practice of immersion was replaced by wetting the baby's head with water from the font, from which we get our saying. This sanctified font water was credited with magical powers which enabled it to cure toothache, amongst other assorted ailments. In many churches font water had to be kept under lock and key, away from those who would use it to practise witchcraft. For the christening of the Princess Royal, Victoria, which took place on the first wedding anniversary of Queen Victoria and Prince Albert, a special golden lily font was made and the baby was anointed with water from the River Jordan, a custom which went back to the days of the crusades.

In Ancient Rome the *lustratio* was the day set aside for naming the new baby and establishing its parentage. This day usually occurred nine days after the birth of a boy and eight days after the birth of a girl. The ceremony took place at the house of the parents and was attended by friends and relations, but not usually the mother, who would still be confined to her rooms. In a wealthy home the nurse would lay the baby at the feet of the father who acknowledged his offspring, and therefore its legitimacy, by raising the child and naming him or her at the same time. Gifts were given to the child by the visitors and a feast followed.

The feast is an integral part of every ceremony, religious or secular. The wealthy landowner or feudal lord of medieval Europe would offer free wine at the birth of his child, especially if that child was male. Once his child was christened and out of the devil's way, for the time being anyway, the landowner used the feast which followed the christening as an opportunity to grant requests and pardon those who had fallen foul of him. In medieval France the *baptême* also fulfilled the function of acknowledging the child's legitimacy, and therefore settled any disputes regarding inheritance of lands and titles.

Even into the eighteenth century, christening feasts in rural England

*Religious subjects were popular in the late eighteenth and early nineteenth centuries. This one called* The Christening *was painted by Francis Wheatley (1747–1801)*

A Scottish Christening
*by John Philip (1817–67)*

involved the whole village, with a hierarchy amongst the diners: those with plenty of children had the finest utensils with which to eat, those with few children had less elaborate utensils and bachelors with no children at all had simple wooden knives and forks.

In the north of England christenings called for a 'groaning board' weighed down with food, particularly cheese and cake. This could be an enormous expense for the parents if they were not well off, but the guests, having stuffed themselves and taken home with them as much as they could carry, made a collection for their hosts. Christenings were not the sedate affairs of today. In the past they were often quite rowdy, the welcome excuse for a party in an age when leisure time was not encouraged.

Eighteenth- and nineteenth-century christenings amongst the wealthy in Europe were elaborate affairs with no expense spared on the clothing of the

child and the dinner which would be given after the church service at the home of the parents. Elegant invitations were sent out, and the dinner menu was printed on special cards as a permanent souvenir of the occasion. The baby, who may have been taken off to bed by his nurse, was toasted by the godparents and close family members around the table.

The choice of godparents reflected a family's social position within the community, while the parents could congratulate themselves if a member of the royal family consented to be a godparent. A royal godparent would expect to have considerable say in the naming of the child. Queen Victoria was to

*The christening of Alfred Duke of Edinburgh at Buckingham Palace, 1874. The nurse with her streamers stands waiting to receive the child. The Queen and Prince Albert and their family stand on the right*

have been called Alexandrina Georgiana, after one godfather, the Tsar of Russia, and after the other, the Prince Regent. However, the Prince disliked his name being after that of the Tsar and since the parents were set on Alexandrina he finally gave his consent to the name Victoria.

When Princess Margaret was born in 1930, she was to have been called Ann Margaret but King George V was not in favour of this and instead her name was changed to Margaret Rose. Today there are many women named Margaret Rose who are all about the same age as the Princess. Edward VIII was named Edward Albert Christian George Andrew Patrick David, the last four names being those of the patron saints of England, Scotland, Ireland and Wales.

Names were thought to have enormous significance, especially in tribal communities when the elderly, being wiser in these matters, would be asked to name the child. The name given to the newborn was thought to affect the

*Mrs Cory-Wright's twin sons were christened in May 1925 in Eaton Square, London*

way in which he lived his life, so names were chosen with great care. To North American Indians the naming of a child meant that the qualities of the person after whom the child was named would pass on to the child. However, some tribes chose not to name their offspring until they had reached six or seven years of age, in order to discover the qualities that would distinguish the child from the rest of the tribe, and thus assist in the selection of a name. To fool the spirits the Japanese would give their children temporary names for the first few weeks.

Events in the past influenced the names of children. During the French Revolution children were dedicated to the state and commissioners stood in as the equivalent of godparents. These babies were called such names as Lycurgus, Fructidor, Constitution, République, Egalité and Epaminodes. It is recorded that early Americans named their children Kill-Sin and Joy-From-Above.

A number of more popular names have distant associations with the Nativity. Noël, or Noëlle, means a child born at Christmas time, as does Natalie or Nathalie from the Latin *dies natalis* (birthday of the Lord). The word 'star' gives us Estelle and Stella, and the angels were represented by Angelina, Angela or Angel for a boy or girl. Holly is for the plant associated with Christmas; Carol or Carola are for the songs sung at that time of year; and Felicity and Felix are representative of the happy tidings brought about with the birth of Christ, from which we take the names Christopher, Christian and Christina.

In the twentieth century names no longer hold the significance that they once did in the past. *The Nursery World* published an article in 1926 proclaiming that 'society is positively drowning under a deluge of Aprils, Mays and Junes, Jeans, Betties and Dianas.'

Associations with nature are often suggested, particularly with girls' names such as Hazel, Olive, Rosemary, Poppy, Heather, Cherry, Primrose, Rose, Marigold, Holly, Daisy and Iris. Months of the year – Augusta, June, April and May – and even a day of the week – Tuesday – have served as Christian names for thousands of women.

Fashions in names were generated by the film stars of the 1940s who, incidentally, often changed their own names to something the movie studio felt was more appealing to the general public. Lots of little girls grew up in the 1950s and 1960s in America and England named Betty, Fae, Marilyn,

Ginger, Joan, Barbara and Rita, while boys were called Elvis and Gary, or John, George, Paul and even Ringo (one baby was called by all four names of the Beatles). Films produced fashions for names as they did for clothes, such as Scarlett, Melanie or even Tara, from Margaret Mitchell's *Gone with the Wind*.

Children have been named after winning football teams, whole or in part, and famous statesmen such as Winston Churchill and George Washington. Recently, after the signing of a non-proliferation agreement concerning nuclear arms, one mother of twins named her sons Mikail, after the General Secretary of the USSR, Mikail Gorbachev, and Ronald, after the United States President, Ronald Reagan. Another new mother thought that the hospital had named her daughter when she read the name tag around the little girl's wrist – 'Noname'.

Choosing a name can be an extraordinarily difficult task in some families. There is often a great deal of pressure to name the infant, especially if it is a boy, after a dead relative, or after the father or grandfather in the family. Some people choose names seemingly without much thought for their meanings, such as Holly Berry and Sterling Silver, while others give a child far more names than she or he could ever need in a lifetime, thus providing the child with an endless source of embarrassment.

Some families like to choose the name of a man or woman who appears in the Bible as a Christian name for their children. Catholic families often include the name of a saint either as the first or second name. Some of the more popular saints' names and their saints' days follow: Adrian (8 September), Agatha (5 February), Agnes (21 January), Andrew (30 November), Anne (26 July), Anthony (13 June), Barbara (4 December), Beatrice (29 July), Bernard (20 August), Bridget (8 October), Catherine (25 November), Cecilia (22 November), Christina (24 July), Christopher (25 July), Clare (12 August), Edward (13 October), Elizabeth (19 November), Francis (4 October), George (23 April), Gregory (17 June), Henry (15 July), Hilary (14 January), James (25 July), Lawrence (10 August), Lucy (13 December), Margaret (20 July), Mark (25 April), Martha (29 July), Matthew (21 September), Nicholas (6 December), Patrick (17 March), Paul (26 June), Philip (11 May), Simon (28 October), Susanna (11 August), Teresa (15 October), Victor (28 July), Vincent (22 January) and William (25 June).

Gifts also feature in the baptism and christening ceremonies, traditionally

*Three sixteenth-century apostle spoons:* left to right *St James the Great, St John the Evangelist, St Bartholomew*

*A silver-gilt christening set, comprising a beaker decorated with a band of bacchanalian infants and a circular dish with a vine border, and a cast vine pattern spoon, knife and fork. The knife and fork are inscribed 'To Victor Christian William Cavendish from his Godmother Victoria R.' and dated 25 June 1868*

given by godparents and guests. In the past the recipients included not only the baby but also its nurse and other children in the family. The first recorded presents were money, salt and food. According to the American writer, Barbara Tuchman, in the spring of 1367 a daughter, Philippa, was born to Enguerrand de Coucy and his wife Isabella of England. The baby's royal grandparents gave her a silver service of six gilded and chased bowls, six cups, four water pitchers and four platters. She also received twenty-four dishes, twenty-four salt cellars (salt being in great use as a preservative), and twenty-four spoons. The total cost of the gift amounted to £230 18s 3d.

Silverware, in the form of spoons, became the traditional christening gift in medieval times. Spoons had made their appearance on the dining table a little later than knives and were treasured household objects. Forks came into existence much later. Silver spoons could be given only by the wealthy, hence the expression to be born with a silver spoon in one's mouth.

Spoons were considered to be an art form in their own right by the late 1600s, made by silversmiths, while knives were made by master cutlers. The knobs soon became the most interesting aspect of the spoon, being designed to represent one of the apostles, and between the sixteenth and nineteenth centuries sets of apostle spoons became popular as gifts to the new baby. The top of each spoon depicts a saint holding an implement, most often: St Peter carries a key or a fish; St John is shown with a chalice, an eagle or a palm branch; St Andrew holds a saltire cross; St James the Greater is shown with a

*A selection of christening gifts from Tiffany and Co, New York*

130

staff; St James the Less has a fuller's bat because he was killed by a blow on the head by Simeon the Fuller; St Philip bears a staff or a basket of bread; St Bartholomew has a butcher's knife; St Simon Zelotes has a long saw; St Thomas holds a spear; St Matthias or St Thaddeus is shown with a cross or a club; St Matthew carries an axe and St Paul carries a sword.

As christening gifts, spoons were often accompanied by silver cups, bowls and goblets. Today the 'porringer' remains as a traditional christening gift. Queen Mary gave Prince Charles, her great-grandson, a silver gilt cup which George III, her great-grandfather, had given to a godson in 1780. By the nineteenth century many cups were ornate and elaborately decorated, often reflecting the interests and hobbies of the parents by depicting hunting scenes, for example, but others were designed with children in mind and showed scenes from fairy stories or nursery rhymes. The New York store, Tiffany, was famous for its elaborately decorated christening cups.

Napkin rings engraved with the child's name, silver brush and comb sets ($1.20c in a box ordered from the 1902 Sears catalogue) and rattles, were other acceptable gifts. Many rattles were made of mother-of-pearl, with silver bells and whistles or 'whissles' as they were known, coral or ivory on which the child could suck. In the late nineteenth century Punch-head rattles enjoyed a vogue amongst the wealthy.

The other most important aspect to the christening was the robes worn by the infant. At a time when all children were swaddled, the problem of removing the baby's bindings at the font was solved by taking the child naked to his christening, wrapped in a bearing cloth or cloak. In the fifteenth century this cloth was often made of velvet, and in the sixteenth century when the heavy Venetian needlepoint laces became fashionable, it was trimmed and decorated. The robes were often so long and cumbersome that several attendants would be required to carry them, rather like a bridal train. Undoubtedly royal babies had the longest cloaks, made of purple cloth.

The 'chrisom' cloak, as it was also known, became increasingly elaborate over the centuries, and when the practice of immersion ceased, and the baby was no longer required to attend the ceremony naked, he or she was dressed in long robes instead. Godparents made gifts of christening shifts to new parents in some cases, but in general every parent of modest means would struggle to purchase the materials necessary to make a formal christening dress, petticoats and a cap.

It is impossible to write about infant christening robes without considering the history of lace and the role it played in adorning baby clothes. Many writers, including this one, have attempted to define lace. It is one of the more complex fabrics, taking various forms, which makes definition complicated. Lace is a decorative fabric and it is worth pointing out that it is not the exclusive fabric of the wealthy. Rich and poor alike have used it in their homes and on their persons. As a form of decoration, lace, in some cases, has changed little over a hundred years, while in other instances it has been a subject of fashion, constantly changing and evolving.

Lace is made either by needlepoint or by the use of bobbins but it is possible to find items in museums which reveal that both methods were employed together. Early needlelace, or needlepoint lace, dating from the fifteenth and sixteenth centuries, was created on a woven ground (*réseau*) of buttonhole stitches, the exact form and shape of which depended, in a historical context, on the place and time when the lace was made. Bobbin lace was made by using bobbins, small pieces of bone, wood or brass with threads attached to them. The pattern of the lace was picked out by pins and the lace was created by manoeuvring the bobbin threads, rather like weaving, around each other.

Fashions in lace have fluctuated in the same manner as other fabrics, dependent upon the silhouette, design and texture of fabrics in vogue at any given time. However, lace used on baby clothing was not subject to fashion's whim in the same way, since only certain laces were appropriate for decorating baby clothes. These laces were those that could be worked on a small scale, such as Buckinghamshire, Bedfordshire and 'Hollie point' lace from England, and Brussels, Valenciennes, Torchon and the novelty Maltese lace from the Continent. The origins of the name 'Hollie point' are various. Some writers have suggested that it is a derivative of the word 'Holy' and that it was once a lace used to decorate ecclesiastical gowns, but a more mundane origin is likely. Hollie point was one of the most commonly used laces on christening gowns throughout the nineteenth century.

The lace decorations on christening robes were usually restricted to the neck, quite often the yoke, the front panel of the dress, the hem and the sleeve edgings, although some ensembles were extremely elaborate with lace dresses actually being worn over silk slips, rather like contemporary bridal dresses. From the mid-nineteenth century Ayrshire work was enormously popular in

*A cotton lawn christening robe from the second half of the nineteenth century. A short-sleeved bodice with a scalloped frill of fine cotton hand-embroidered in white thread; overstitched at the point where the frill is sewn to the sleeve in featherstitch; round neckline edged in cotton lace. The dress has a long back opening which fastens with narrow cotton tape at the neck and at the waist, the skirt gathered to the waist by tiny pleats. The skirt is decorated with a central panel of alternate rows of pin-tucks and strips of embroidered lawn. The garment is completely hand sewn*

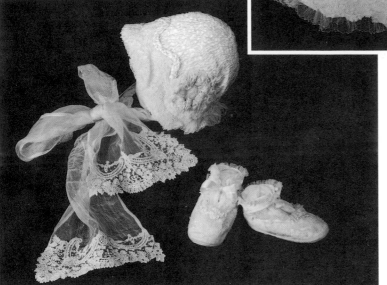

*The Valentine Museum in Richmond, Virginia, holds a unique christening dress designed by the Paris fashion house of Worth in 1924. At the time the outfit cost Mr Campbell Dierks, the prospective father, $2,000. It is enormously elaborate, being made of fine handkerchief linen which is trimmed with rosepoint lace. Tiny pearl buttons close the shoulders. The slip is of fine white satin and the cape and cap are made of silk faille, with rosepoint trim, the cap having rosettes and chiffon strings with lace ends. The shoes are made also of silk faille, trimmed with rosepoint lace, and they have a rosette on the vamp, ankle straps and round toes, with satin ties and leather soles. The christening outfit is believed to be the only one made by the House of Worth.*

England for baptismal clothing. Ayrshire work consisted of small embroidered floral motifs which had cutwork centres and needlepoint lace fillings.

The christening gown would be the most expensive item made for the newborn baby, regardless of whether the lace was made by hand or, in the second half of the nineteenth century, by machine, which is probably why so many christening robes were passed down from one generation to the next. Tradition plays a role in this also. All Queen Victoria's children wore the same christening gown which was created for Vicky, the Princess Royal, using the work of the Honiton lacemakers that the Queen had commissioned for her wedding dress in 1840. Honiton lace was seldom used for trimmings of babies' clothes but it has strong associations with the British royal family.

Most nineteenth-century christening ensembles comprised of the following: a slip of muslin or satin with its own decorative trim on the sleeves, neck and hem; a dress of linen or cotton, with lace, and/or *embroiderie anglais* inserts; a cape which was often tied with ribbons; a cap; and matching bootees.

Styles in christening robes mirrored fashion but at a much slower pace. Most common was the dress with an Empire line and yoke but in the late nineteenth century, the Princess line was one of the most distinctive changes, as its waistless cut and flowing lines suited baby very well.

An extremely unusual christening gown is in the possession of the Museum of the City of New York. It was believed to have been made around 1855 for the exposition at the Crystal Palace in New York, where it was purchased. Heavily embroidered with Ayrshire work, the dress features a number of motifs not usually associated with infancy such as cannons, goats and the seal of the city of New York. Other motifs include birds, flowers and the Union shield.

Lace insertions on christening dresses were occasionally formed into words, such as 'Long Live the Babe', rather like the mottos found on baby pillows, but more usually the motifs were flowers, particularly the lily, the *fleur de lis*, the lamb, the dove, birds and even squirrels.

No.38R1412 Infants' All Wool Flannel Hand Embroidered Shawl, elaborately embroidered with silk in a very pretty flower design, scalloped and stitched with silk. Exceptionally good value.
    Price. **$1.19  If by mail, postage extra, 6 cents.**

No.38R1370 Infants' Long Skirt, made of fine nainsook, trimmed with three clusters (four rows in a cluster) of fine tucks with two rows of Valenciennes insertion. Trimmed around the bottom with wide Valenciennes lace to match. A very pretty and attractive skirt.
    Price, each. **$1.48  If by mail, postage extra, 8 cents.**

*Just two of Sears Roebuck's infant clothing advertised in their catalogue of 1902*

When she reached home it was to learn to her grief that the baby had been suddenly taken ill since the afternoon. Some such collapse had been probable, so tender and puny was its frame; but the event came as a shock nevertheless.

The baby's offence against society in coming into the world was forgotten by the girl-mother; her soul's desire was to continue that offence by preserving the life of the child. However, it soon grew clear that the hour of emancipation for that little prisoner of the flesh was to arrive earlier than her worst misgivings had conjectured. And when she had discovered this she was plunged into a misery which transcended that of the child's simple loss. Her baby had not been baptized . . .

It was nearly bedtime, but she rushed downstairs and asked if she might send for the parson. The moment happened to be one at which her father's sense of the antique nobility of his family was highest, and his sensitiveness to the smudge which Tess had set upon that nobility most pronounced, for he had just returned from his weekly booze at Rolliver's Inn. No parson should come inside his door, he declared, prying into his affairs, just then, when, by her shame, it had become more necessary than ever to hide them. He locked the door and put the key in his pocket.

The household went to bed, and, distressed beyond measure, Tess retired also. She was continually waking as she lay, and in the middle of the night found that the baby was still worse. It was obviously dying – quietly and painlessly, but none the less surely . . .

She leant against the chest of drawers, and murmured incoherent supplications for a long while, till she suddenly started up.

'Ah! perhaps baby can be saved! Perhaps it will be just the same!' . . .

She lit a candle, and went to a second and a third bed under the wall, where she awoke her young sisters and brothers, all of whom occupied the same room. Pulling out the washing-stand so that she could get behind it, she poured some water from a jug, and made them kneel around, putting their hands together with fingers exactly vertical. While the children, scarcely awake, awe-stricken at her manner, their eyes growing larger and larger, remained in this position, she took the baby from her bed – a child's child – so immature as scarce to seem a sufficient personality to endow its producer with the maternal title. Tess then stood erect with the infant on her arm beside the basin, the next sister held the Prayer Book open before her, as the clerk at church held it before the parson; and thus the girl set about baptizing her child . . .

'Be you really going to christen him, Tess?'

The girl-mother replied in a grave affirmative.

'What's his name going to be?'

She had not thought of that, but a name suggested by a phrase in the book of Genesis came into her head as she proceeded with the baptismal service, and now she pronounced it:

WETTING THE BABY'S HEAD

'SORROW, I baptize thee in the name of the Father, and of the Son, and of the Holy Ghost.'

She sprinkled the water, and there was silence.

'Say "Amen", children.'

The tiny voices piped in obedient response 'Amen!'

Tess went on:

'We receive this child' – and so forth – 'and do sign him with the sign of the Cross.'

Here she dipped her hand into the basin, and fervently drew an immense cross upon the baby with her forefinger, continuing with the customary sentences as to his manfully fighting against sin, the world, and the devil, and being a faithful soldier and servant until his life's end. She duly went on with the Lord's Prayer, the children lisping it after her in a thin gnatlike wail, till, at the conclusion, raising their voices to clerk's pitch, they again piped into the silence, 'Amen!' . . .

*Tess of the D'Urbervilles*, Thomas Hardy

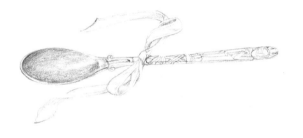

# Plain or Fancy

ALL
GOOD
DRAPERS
SELL
THEM

HARRINGTONS
SQUARES

THE way in which we dress our children is a reflection not only of the social attitudes of the time, but of our economic situations. A well-dressed baby is a symbol of family wealth and mother's pride. Even people who have been hard pressed to find clothing for their children laboured to maintain the traditional white fabrics for the baby to wear. In medieval times fabric which we would today consider totally unsuitable for children, such as velvet, plush, silk and fur, was used for cloaks, coverlets and crib furnishings by those who could afford it, while everyone else used linen.

As all babies were swaddled, so that they looked like some sort of animated sleeping bag, the necessity for individual garments to clothe infants, as we know them today, did not exist. There were names for various items in which the baby was swaddled and made immobile. One such item was a 'Pilch', made from a square of flannel or other material. Pilches were worn under the swaddling bands, and later clothes, to prevent wetness soaking through. Another item was the 'barrow' – a long piece of fabric, flannel or linen, which was wrapped around the baby below the arms with the long part pinned up over the feet.

By Tudor times although people were beginning to deplore the practice of swaddling, preferring simple clothing instead, others put these new items on *under* swaddling clothes. It wasn't until the seventeenth and early eighteenth centuries that swaddling bands went out of favour but in rural parts of the country babies were still being swaddled into the early nineteenth century.

138

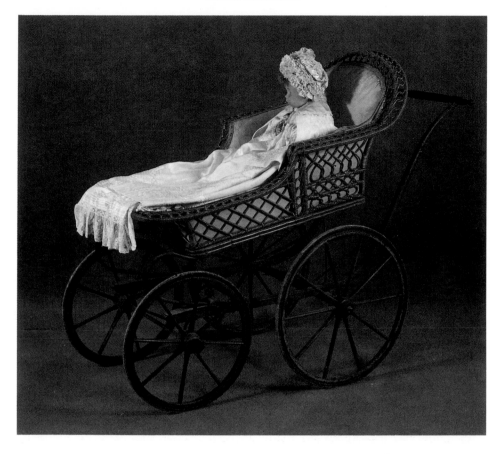

*Baby clothes from the second half of the nineteenth century*

Binders were the relics of swaddling bands. A binder was a band of fabric which was tied around the baby's abdomen to provide warmth, support the back and to protect the dressing on the umbilical cord. During the health cult of the Victorian age these binders were made of wool, and by the 1920s the binder had become a wide flannel belt which was worn around the abdomen beneath the baby's underwear.

Until the end of the eighteenth century there were three stages of children's dress: swaddling clothes; petticoats, which both boys and girls wore up to the age of about two years; and scaled-down versions of adult clothes. There were remarkably few changes in infant fashions over the centuries, with the

exception of the 1900s. Most changes in infant dress occurred when the swaddling bands were left off and the child began to walk. Depending on the dictates of the time, ambulatory infants were put in corded stays which they wore underneath their petticoats and in the sixteenth century infants wore aprons and tall, winged bonnets, as was the fashion of the time.

Throughout the following two centuries, infant clothing mirrored women's clothing in styles but the basic garments, once the swaddling bands had been discarded, remained the same. By the early nineteenth century a baby wore a flannel binder around its stomach, pilches, a nappy, a linen shirt, several long flannel petticoats which reached from the waist to well below the feet (unless the child was learning to walk) and a cotton, linen or muslin gown which, depending on the circumstances of the parents, would be variously embroidered or trimmed on the bodice, the hem and often the sleeves. The baby would wear leather shoes or knitted bootees, depending on the stage of development, and a day cap for indoors, and a bonnet, or cloth cap, often placed on top of the cap, for going outside. At bedtime the cap would be exchanged for a night cap. One or two shawls or receiving blankets would be wrapped around the baby, and if he or she was taken outside a woollen or lace veil would be hung over the bonnet to conceal the face as fresh air was considered harmful for babies.

Until the 1840s practically every garment was made at home by hand. But in the mid-nineteenth century stores calling themselves outfitters sold 'baby linen', along with women's underwear which had also been made exclusively in the home. This baby linen was exactly that, embroidered linens and cottons which could be purchased and made up into coverlets and clothing. With the rise in the 1800s of ready-to-wear clothing, basic baby shifts were available ready-made. The availability of manufactured lace also contributed to the mass-marketing of infant clothing, although most christening robes were still made by hand.

In the last quarter of the nineteenth century a typical robe for a baby would have been made of fine white cotton lawn, with a high gathered neckline which was trimmed with cotton lace. A deep yoke, with a frill of needlepoint lace, had a triangular piece of tucked cotton at the centre which was edged with flounces of cotton. The sleeves were puffed and gathered at the shoulder, ending in similar flounces to the yoke edge. The robe opened at the back where it was gathered and fastened with cotton tapes at neck and waist, and

## TO BABY

Oh, what shall my blue eyes go
see?
Shall it be pretty quack-quack
to-day?
Or the peacock upon the yew
tree?
Or the dear little white lambs
at play?
Say baby.
For baby is such a young petsy,
And baby is such a sweet dear.
And baby is growing quite old
now
She's just getting on for a year.

*Crochet and knitted bonnets have been popular for over 100 years and have changed little in style during that time*

five tiny mother-of-pearl buttons. The bodice was gathered into the waist where rows of thin cord couched on to the waistband gave the effect of smocking. The skirt of the robe was closely pleated into the waist and the lower part of the skirt was decorated with rows of pin-tucking, alternated with rows of feather-stitch embroidery in white cotton. At the hem there was a flounce of lace and tucks. By contrast a poor baby would wear a muslin shift, a short printed cotton robe and a plain muslin cap.

During the Victorian era infant clothing became so complicated and cumbersome that by the 1870s many people were re-thinking the whole idea of what their babies wore. The Rational Dress Society, founded in 1881, turned to the problem of infant clothing and recommended that long dresses should be shortened so as not to hinder the child's movement. The recommended layette consisted of four fine woollen binders, four little woollen vests, four robes of flannel or cashmere, two day gowns, two head flannels, and forty-eight Turkish towelling nappies. However, real change in infant clothing did not come about until the post-First-World-War years of the twentieth century.

Many examples of nineteenth-century baby clothes exist in museums in Europe but they are often difficult to date because styles have changed so little. Knitted garments, while recorded as being in use in the sixteenth century for adults, were unlikely to have been worn by babies as the finer yarns, needed when working on a small scale, were not known in England until the early eighteenth century.

The use of wool to make babies' clothes was most popular during the Victorian health cult which resulted in wool being used for just about every conceivable garment, including swimwear. The health cult also exposed babies' necks, as the bavalet, the piece of the bonnet which covers the nape of the neck, was discarded once and for all. The idea behind this practice was to 'toughen up' the baby, in complete contrast to the previous centuries when people abhorred the idea of exposing their infants to the elements.

Until fairly recently in our history a bare-headed baby would have been an unusual sight. Even the poorest parents would find a scrap of linen out of which they could create a small close-fitting cap, while those babies born to wealthy families had versions made in silk and trimmed with lace. These babies would also have had day and night caps, as well as a wardrobe of bonnets and hoods.

The most simple form of the cap, in use for centuries, was a piece of linen, cotton or muslin, seamed in two or three sections, which covered the baby's ears. Caps were worn by both boys and girls. Baptismal and christening caps were more elaborate and trimmed in a similar manner to the robes with which they were worn. Depending on the fabric of the robe, caps were made from cotton, silk, lawn or muslin and trimmed with lace frills. Late seventeenth- and early eighteenth-century caps were often beautifully embroidered with the designs marked out first in pencil.

Styles varied very little: some caps had a crown shaped by gathering the material across the back and in the nineteenth century they were known as 'foundling' caps; others were gathered to a central point on top of the head and shirred; most were made in two sections (a crown and a lower section), or three bands, the narrowest going from the centre back of the neck to the forehead. Many caps had insertions of the traditional baby lace, Hollie point, which ran from the front over the top of the head to the back. Beautiful caps of Valenciennes lace or Buckinghamshire pillow lace were worn on their own or placed over a little muslin under-cap. With the availability of machine-made lace in the nineteenth century caps became increasingly elaborate with profusions of lace trimmings. Rosettes of satin were sewn on to the left-hand side of a cap for a boy, and to the right-hand side for a girl. Knitted caps, some made with geometric patterns worked in beads, became popular during the late nineteenth century and this trend continued through the 1950s with

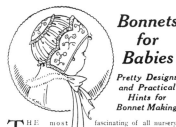

## Bonnets for Babies

*Pretty Designs and Practical Hints for Bonnet Making*

THE most fascinating of all nursery garments to make are, perhaps, the bonnets. For one thing, they are small enough to be quickly finished, a great point in their favour to those who are just setting forth on a sewing career.

Do remember when making a bonnet how much depends upon the *strings*, not only the quality of the ribbon—it will pay you in the long run to get good quality ribbon for it will never split or get "stiff" with repeated washings like the cheap varieties—but upon the position in which they are sewn. See that they are perfectly comfortably placed.

I recommend the bottom bonnet for the very beginner to try her 'prentice hand" on. This is a crocheted one of shell stitch. The swansdown can be omitted and a simple crochet edging substituted if something simpler is liked. There's a Russian influence about the

other bonnet. The model was in sky blue crêpe de Chine, embroidered in ivory silk and edged with white marabout—which will, by the way, wash quite well, in warm soapy water, then dried, not too quickly, with many and vigorous shakings. It is always advisable to use a little stiffening for bonnet turn-backs. Book muslin is just the right texture for this sort of thing. Ribbed silk—we knew it years ago as "bengaline"—makes delicious little bonnets to be worn with lamb's-wool, cloth, or the thicker silk coats; and the artist has drawn the one in the heading for this material.

The front has a scalloped turn-back and is also embroidered and then edged with gathered val lace.

A very "first" bonnet is the one with the choux. This could be made in ribbon entirely in different widths — remnants from the bargain counters at the sales—for sales are very happy hunting grounds for mothers of families and remnant days real "money-savers" where bonnets and other tiny garments are concerned.

*Grass hat worn by a Spanish baby in 1907, made of coiled straw held together with twine and lined with glazed cotton and edged with pink ribbon*

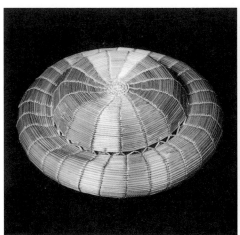 

143

numerous pattern books being produced giving instructions for knitted baby caps.

The old-fashioned name for a baby's bonnet was a 'biggin'. Bonnets were worn when the baby went out, just as a woman wore a cap in the house but a bonnet if she went out; however, there are many irregularities in these descriptions with caps referred to as bonnets and vice versa. More than any other item of infant dress, bonnets more closely mirrored the fashions worn by women: when the poke bonnet went out of fashion for women, so it was seen less on babies, and when the cloche hat of the 1920s was popular babies wore versions of it also. The early Dutch settlers in the USA dressed their babies in their own particular style of bonnet. When the Princess Royal was taken out in the 1840s, she wore a white muslin dress and a Quaker bonnet, as was the style at the time.

Bonnets could be plain, printed, rucked, shirred, gathered and adorned with lace. Many were trimmed with ostrich feathers but more often than not they were covered with masses of lace, and they tied under the chin with satin ties. Fabrics such as satin, organdie and straw were used as well as linen, cotton, cashmere, serge, lawn, silk, Shetland wool and knitted lisle.

Baby hoods became popular about one hundred years ago and they can still be seen today. The hood is a one-piece garment, a hood-like bonnet with a flowing cap attached. In the late nineteenth century and early twentieth century many hoods, or cappets as they were also known, were made in merino, cashmere and kerseymere, and they were worn over a day cap. In the 1950s the hood was a popular feature in knitting pattern books.

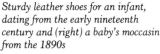

*Sturdy leather shoes for an infant, dating from the early nineteenth century and (right) a baby's moccasin from the 1890s*

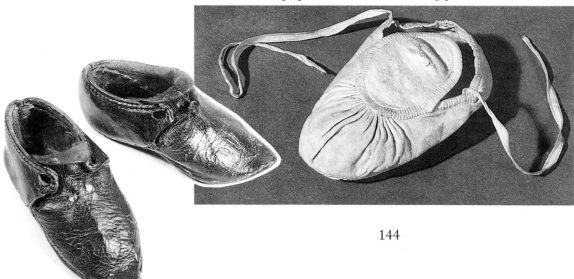

144

*A pair of twentieth-century
Chinese baby's shoes for
mutilated feet, in
embroidered pink satin*

Infant headgear not only acted as protection against the sun, rain and wind. The hats and caps worn by people in the East often reflected the status of the family and therefore the child within the tribe. The symbols which are sewn into the material were intentions of how the child should live his life and, in some tribes, those same symbols would be worked into the materials which surrounded the person when his life finally came to an end. Many of the signs were designed to ward off the Evil Eye, while others were believed to have powers to attract good spirits, spirits representing health, wealth and promise of great achievement.

In some parts of the world shoes were also the objects of superstitious symbolism. In Korea infants wore shoes that were deliberately too large for them. This symbolized growth and long life. In China, tiger imagery was embroidered on to shoes to protect the child from demons. In Europe infants were put into extraordinarily lavish shoes and bootees, many of which were never seen under the long robes. The amount of detail that went into creating the shoes, especially shoes that might not be seen very often, tells us how people felt about their infants. One pair of shoes, existing from the nineteenth century, has the words 'My mother made these for me' stitched to the soles, which each measure about four inches. It was impossible to tell if the shoe was supposed to fit the left or right foot. Many shoes were made of silk and satin, which would have been fine, if the child wasn't learning to walk. Infants' shoes imitated children's shoes, which in turn imitated adult shoes, like the Mary Jane style, with a strap across the ankle, which was popular in the early twentieth century.

*A pair of baby's shoes in red and yellow satin representing a fish*

It wasn't until much later, however, after the Second World War that people began to pay attention to what they put on their children's feet. Although infants had been wearing sturdy leather shoes for centuries, and there was some acknowledgement to the importance of footwear in the late nineteenth century, it was during the 1950s that the firm little 'Jumping Jacks', and other shoes, were designed which supported the feet. Soon, people were buying shoes that they hoped would help their child's feet to grow properly over the years, although, of course, during the 1960s, all good intentions gave way to fashion, even for babies, in the clothing revolution that took place during that decade. At this time the knitted woollen bootees were made of acrylic mixtures and other man-made fibres.

Perhaps the most remarkable thing about eighteenth- and nineteenth-century infant clothing is the amount of work, thought and care that went into its creation. Not only did the lace have to be made, before machine-made examples were readily available, but all the seams were sewn by hand as well as the embroidery and other trimmings. One imagines that it was not only tradition that stipulated the handing-down of christening dresses from one generation to the next; it would have taken weeks of work to make just one of the elaborate robes worn by babies.

The first half of the twentieth century brought many changes in infant clothing. The Princess and Empire lines of the previous century were still popular for robes but along with new concepts in bringing up children came

new ideas in dress. The most important change was that people no longer found it shocking to see their infants crawl. To many Victorians, the sight of crawling infants reminded them of their ape-like origins, and they forced their children to learn to walk with the aid of cages and walkers, besides which, those delicately embroidered dresses could not have withstood the antics of an eight-month-old baby who was determined to investigate the world at ground level. Books recommended putting babies in short clothes from the age of eight or nine months so that they might crawl. The range of suitable clothing suggested for infants included petticoats, shorter dresses, drawers, pinafores and laced shoes or boots. For the first time, infant clothing was shortened to allow the baby to move freely, with longer robes being reserved for formal occasions such as christenings and the presentation of the baby to the grandparents.

Since the late nineteenth century stores and mail-order catalogues had been selling ready-made infant clothing, and the range of styles available increased during the following century, although the demand for traditional clothing continued for some time. In Europe so-called American lines were popular, while in the USA people wanted clothes designed in France and trimmed with French lace, or made from fine English fabrics. In 1909, the London store of Dickins & Jones was offering muslin matinée jackets which were trimmed with lace and embroidery of silk, slips to be worn under christening gowns and caps made in muslin, which could be purchased trimmed in imitation Valenciennes lace, torchon or real Valenciennes. Another London store, the Army & Navy, offered silk cream jackets trimmed with lace, cashmere cloaks, cream alpaca jackets which were trimmed with jap silk embroidery, flannel head squares, muslin and piqué cloaks and crochet jackets. Some of the infant gowns sold were hand-made, others were machine-made with real lace insertions.

*An early twentieth-century infant outfit available from the London store of Army & Navy*

From the 1920s infants were wearing two rather than four layers of clothing. Dresses were much shorter and more likely to button at the front. Perhaps the most popular item was the infant vest. In 1902 the American mail-order giant Sears, Roebuck sold the Reuben's Infant Shirt which was made of '66⅔ per cent fine wool with straps and a small safety pin', and otherwise no fastenings. Sears' Derby Ribbed Cream wool vests and white merino wool and cotton mix vests were popular. By the 1950s in England the

147

Chilprufe vest, available in a variety of styles, was one of the best known.

Other than vests, sleeping suits, rompers, diaper suits and crawling suits replaced binders, chemises, petticoats and long dresses. The all-in-one diaper suit had, in fact, been worn by babies since the eighteenth century but in the early twentieth century it started to resemble more closely the items worn by babies today. By the 1950s American diaper pants and rompers had words

*A spread of baby clothes from a 1950s knitting magazine*

DIRECTIONS, SEE NEXT PAG

embroidered across the backs, such as 'My First Christmas', 'Don't Spank', and 'Baby'.

Although a great many infant clothes were redesigned during the mid-war years, it was during the 1950s that the greatest changes took place. More than ever before coloured clothing was seen. The traditional white robes were reserved for christenings, with the occasional 'candlelight' robe, a soft burnished cream colour which was favoured in the 1890s, being seen, but for everyday wear infants were now dressed in pastels of every shade, no longer with pink trimmings for girls and blue for boys. In the 1980s certain designers are advocating putting infants and toddlers in black and white patterned clothes but they are meeting some resistance from parents.

Infant fashions of the 1950s copied those of adults. The artifice and heavy decoration disappeared to be replaced with clothing that looked both functional and fun. Pockets and buttons were featured in design and collars were typical of the period, being wide and flat. Smocking, which had been in use during the nineteenth century, became fashionable once again. Like their mothers, infants wore outfits, with matching gloves and boots. Cardigan sets and leggings were often knitted or crocheted.

It was during this decade that the motifs on infant clothing became far more visible, often integral parts of the design of the outfit. The motifs we take for granted today, such as nautical themes of boats and anchors, or borders of trains and cars, or flowers, birds and farm animals such as roosters and ducks, were applied increasingly during the 1950s and 1960s. Infantwear designers became more adventurous in their choices of fabric, using many of the new man-made fibres and making complete outfits out of gingham. It was during the 1960s that plastic was used in clothing for both babies and adults. The 1960s will also be remembered in history as the unisex decade when little girls were dressed in little boys' clothes. In 1962 the one-piece Babygro stretch suit, invented by Walter Artat in New York, was launched and by the end of the decade the garment had become a household name.

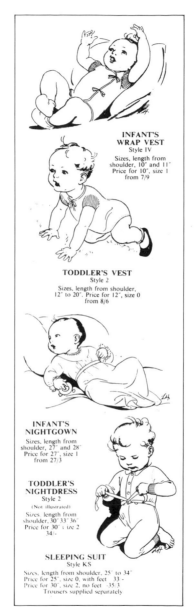

**INFANT'S WRAP VEST**
Style IV
Sizes, length from shoulder, 10" and 11"
Price for 10", size 1 from 7/9

**TODDLER'S VEST**
Style 2
Sizes, length from shoulder, 12" to 20". Price for 12", size 0 from 8/6

**INFANT'S NIGHTGOWN**
Sizes, length from shoulder, 27" and 28"
Price for 27", size 1 from 27/3

**TODDLER'S NIGHTDRESS**
Style 2
(Not illustrated)
Sizes, length from shoulder, 30" 33" 36"
Price for 30" size 2 34/-

**SLEEPING SUIT**
Style KS
Sizes, length from shoulder, 25" to 34"
Price for 25", size 0, with feet 33 -
Price for 30", size 2, no feet -35/3
Trousers supplied separately

*A selection of items from an early Chilprufe catalogue*

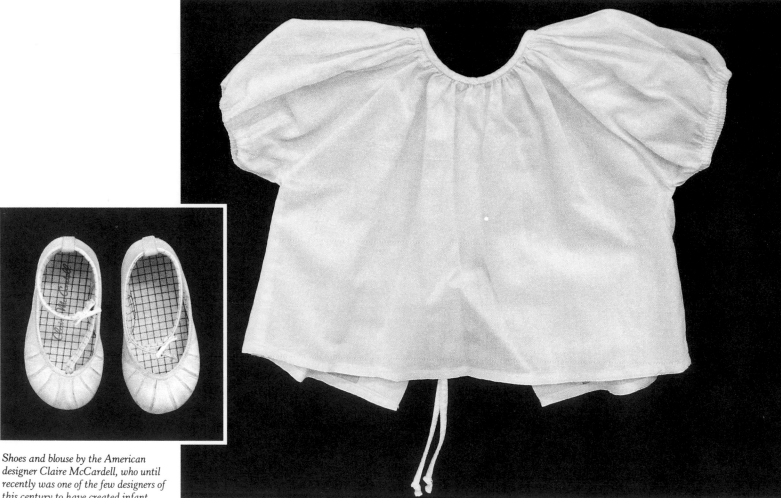

*Shoes and blouse by the American designer Claire McCardell, who until recently was one of the few designers of this century to have created infant fashions*

During the following years boutiques specializing in selling expensive infant clothing have opened all over the world. If they can afford it, people will spend large sums of money on dressing their children in designer outfits for much the same reasons as parents in other centuries clothed their offspring in silk, fur and yard upon yard of hand-made lace. One imagines that it will never be any different.

150

# Under the Cabbage Patch

Augustus John Cecil Hughes spent most of his half-term holiday wishing he was back at school. Here, at home, there was no one to talk to. The servants treated him as if he was still wearing short trousers, he rarely saw his parents and his old nanny, who was brought out of retirement from her home in the country to keep an eye on her former charge, was too old and slow to be of much use to him. Blowing and puffing with exertion, Nanny Smith arrived at Paddington, on the 3.40, fussing over him and smelling of *eau de violette* – 'my parfam', she called it, and that's what he called it too, until his father corrected him when he inquired about his mother's 'parfam'.

No, Nanny was no good any more. He liked her well enough, she didn't mind giving you a hug when you wanted one, but she wasn't interested in his games and she didn't know anything about battleships. In school, at least, there were people to talk to: Brancaster, Smythe, and even old Britchett was worth the time of day if one was feeling in a good mood, such as when one had received good marks in Latin, or been excused games.

Memories of school had made Master Hughes forget where he was. A sudden noise, the sound of a door closing somewhere beneath him, brought his attention back to his sur-roundings and on his stomach he wriggled closer to the hole in the floor through which he had a bird's eye view of the room below.

One afternoon, when Nanny was taking her usual nap by the nursery fire, unable to fend off the effects of the heat after one of cook's more than ample lunches, her jowls slumped on to her chest so that she looked as if God had forgotten to give her a neck, Master Hughes decided it was time to investigate the rest of the house. He rarely had the opportunity to be alone; at school there were boys nudging at his elbows, the inquiring glances of his teachers, or worse, the headmaster, and at home a servant always seemed to appear from nowhere to supervise his every move. But with Louise safely back downstairs in the kitchen with the lunch trays and Nanny asleep he was free to do as he pleased.

The whereabouts of his parents did not concern him. He had never seen his father before six o'clock in the evening. He remembered waiting in the drawing room for the clock to chime six, then footsteps would be heard in the hall as Rogers, the butler, opened the door. The two men exchanged pleasantries, while the butler relieved Mr Hughes of his coat and hat. Then the drawing-room door opened and his father walk-ed in. It was the same every day. When

the school bell rang out six chimes, Hughes half expected to see his father walk in through the school gates and up the gravel driveway.

His mother could be anywhere. Out. At home. Taking tea. But she was less of a problem to Hughes. He decided that he would tell her he was looking for a school book, if she discovered him downstairs. That sort of thing always deflected a grown-up's anger.

He found his mother quite by accident. He went downstairs to the second floor, to the room he so much liked because it was used for nothing in particular. Once, someone had stayed there – he'd seen the bed being moved in – and once lots of large trunks filled up the room, but the rest of the time it was used to store furniture – whose furniture he didn't know because he never saw it in any other room in the house. Sometimes he wondered if there was something wrong with the furniture.

He could tell that the parlour maid didn't think much of the furniture because the legs of the tables and chairs were quite thick with dust. He didn't feel very strongly about dust. It came

152

off your clothing if you brushed hard enough, but it had a strong effect on Nanny whose head would shake about vigorously when she heard the word so that her hairpins would slip out of her hair. That was the only problem with the room. If they ever found dust on him he would be forced to confess where he had been hiding so that the parlour maid could be scolded for her laziness.

The hole in the floor had been uncovered by accident. His foot had tripped on a rug and exposed a perfectly round hole, large enough for him to look through comfortably without having to squint. It was close to the hearth and similar to the one through which the gas pipe disappeared into the skirting board.

Peeping through the hole to his mother's parlour below was how he discovered, although he didn't realize it at the time, that he was going to have a brother or a sister. That first time he positioned himself over the hole, his grandmother was taking tea with his mother, a frequent occurrence; so frequent in fact that unlike other boys he knew, his presence was not required every time Grandmama set foot over the threshold.

Grandmama was agitated about something. She drank her tea swiftly, in little sips, banging her cup down on the saucer every time she made a point in the conversation.

'I'm telling you, my dear girl, that you concern yourself far too much with that boy. He's perfectly fine, believe me. Too much fussing over boys isn't good for them. I brought your three brothers into the world so I should know about these things.'

She raised one hand.

'I know Roderic is the exception, but he takes after your father's side of the family, and I daresay that in time he will come around and settle down to work with your father at the bank.'

'But I don't fuss over Augustus,' his mother said, pouring more tea into the cup Grandmama's rapid sips had just drained. 'I just think about him, that's all, about what he'll think of his new sibling.'

'Think!' said his grandmother. 'Why should he think? If it's a boy, he'll have someone to play with, and if it's a girl, well, he won't have to worry because he'll be away at school.'

Grandmama placed her cup down firmly on the table and drew her shawl around her shoulders.

'You should concern yourself more about your own condition. All this unnecessary worry isn't good for the baby.'

Baby! thought Augustus. What baby? He hadn't seen a baby anywhere. He wriggled about on the floor, trying to get a better view of the room.

His grandmother continued.

'I will, of course, send Mrs Floyd to you, nearer the time.'

'That won't be necessary, Mother, thank you,' said his mother, pouring herself more tea. 'We – *I* – have decided to have Dr Armstrong attend me. He saw two of my friends through their last pregnancies.'

Grandmama folded her hands in her lap.

'I might remind you, Penelope, that I find that word most inappropriate. What does your husband say about all this?'

'It was his idea.'

'I might have guessed it. He should never have brought you to live in London. Too much influence in London. Ideas that come and go too fast.'

'But, Mother, *you* live in London.'

'Well, it's different for me.'

Augustus's mother sighed.

'Dr Armstrong has been practising for years. He attended several ladies at the court and he was consulted during Queen Victoria's last pregnancy. He is a most pleasant man. One feels quite at ease in his company, I'm told.'

'At ease? With a man in the room? Next you will be telling me that Mr Hughes intends to be present and that afterwards all three of you will have dinner together.'

Mrs Hughes laughed. 'And why not? Dr Armstrong is most considerate. He gave me a little doll so that I could indicate my symptoms, but after Augustus, I knew already that I was . . . in a delicate condition,' she added hastily.

After Augustus? What did she mean? He wanted to shout down through the peep hole and ask her. What happened after Augustus? He didn't have an opportunity to find out any more because his mother rang the bell for Louise to come and collect the tea tray and the two women changed their conversation.

He thought about what he had overheard but he couldn't say anything to anyone without revealing that he had been eavesdropping. Once he was back at school he forgot the incident.

It wasn't until he came home from school for the end-of-the-term holiday that he discovered the significance of the conversation. His father had him shown straight into the library. Augustus didn't know what to expect. His end-of-term report was quite good, so it couldn't be a punishment.

'Well,' said his father after greeting him warmly, 'you have a little sister.'

'A sister?' he asked. 'A sister where?'

'At the moment she is upstairs in the nursery with Nanny.'

He couldn't imagine a sister. What did she look like? Brancaster had a sister and he said she was horrid, she pinched his cheeks and laughed at him.

'Where is my mother?' he asked.

'Your mother won't be downstairs for a while. She will send for you when she's feeling better. In the meantime, try not to make too much noise on the stairs.'

'Is she ill?'

'Not exactly,' his father said, 'but she has to stay in bed for a few days.'

'How did she get here, this sister?' asked Augustus.

His father coughed.

'Well, now, Augustus, your mother and I arranged this, and well, you see, with the help of Dr Armstrong, your mother . . . well, the stork brought her.'

The stork? What stork?

'Now, I expect that Rogers has had your trunk taken upstairs and Nanny will have tea ready in the nursery.'

He didn't want to go upstairs. A sister. What was he going to say to her?

Of course, he couldn't say anything. When he first saw his sister she was fast asleep in his old crib, a padded bundle covered in white lace. He looked away from her to where Nanny was standing, a big smile on her face.

'Now, be careful, Master John, she's very fragile.'

Nanny need not worry. He had absolutely no intention of going near this creature.

'What's its name?' he asked Nanny.

'It's not an "it", dear,' said Nanny. 'She's a beautiful girl, and her name is Jacqueline.'

Oh no, something French! He would be made to pronounce that name over and over again in class. Monsieur Le Blanc always made boys who had relatives with French names learn to pronounce them correctly. He said one should do it out of respect for the French language.

Jacqueline. He went nearer and peered at her. A red face and thin, wispy black hair. You couldn't even tell that it was a girl.

'Is she going to stay here?' he asked Nanny.

'Why, of course, Master John,' said Nanny bending over the crib. 'This is *your* little sister.'

His little sister. No one had asked him if he wanted one.

'But where did she come from?' he asked.

Nanny ignored his question. Humming to herself she tucked the covers more closely around the baby.

'How did she get here?' he persisted.

'Your mother and father found her under the cabbage patch,' said Nanny straightening up and walking away.

Augustus moved to the nursery window and looked out through the bars on to the garden. He had never seen any babies down there under the bushes. He would have to ask old Leggat, the gardener.

He was about to press Nanny further on the subject when the baby began to cry. A soft hiccoughing sound followed by screaming. It was hard to believe that so much noise could come from so small a thing.

He was pleased to get back to school. Nine boys in his dormitory made less noise than his baby sister. But he had begun to get used to the noise, the funny gurgling sounds and the yells which Nanny said were caused by too much, or too little, food. He had enjoyed watching Nanny dress the little thing, and he marvelled at her tiny hands and feet, the way her head lolled around on her neck and the soft strands of hair that stuck up at odd angles from her head. Sometimes he liked to stay by

155

the crib and watch her sleep. He saw her yawn, although he didn't know how she could be tired as she slept so much, and he laughed when he saw her clench her little fists.

'Look, Nanny,' he said, 'she's going to be a boxer.'

At half term he came home again. Rogers once more showed him into the library where his father stood, dressed from head to foot in black. It took him a while to speak.

'Son, we've lost Jacqueline.'

Lost her? Where did she go?

'She was very sick, and last week she gave up the fight. Both your mother and I are very upset.'

Augustus couldn't seem to understand what his father was saying to him. He had spent the last few weeks learning to pronounce his sister's name in class so that it rolled off his tongue, just like a real Frenchman. 'Jacqueline, la soeur d'Augustus.'

He ran upstairs. Nanny was sleeping by the fire, her chin deep on her chest in the folds of her white uniform. The nursery looked strangely bare. The empty crib had been moved to one corner.

'Nanny!' He pushed her awake.

'Why, Master John,' said Nanny blinking as she focused on him.

'What happened to the baby?' He pointed at the cradle, the tears beginning to squeeze out of his eyes.

Nanny reached out and put her arms around him. 'Now, now, Master John, don't you cry for your little sister. There

was nothing anyone could do for her. Poor little thing.'

'I'm not crying,' said Augustus. 'I just wanted to know where she went, that's all.'

'She went away,' said Nanny, patting his back. 'There, there, don't upset yourself so.'

Augustus pulled away from Nanny.

'You said she came from under the cabbage patch. I'm going to look for her.'

Ignoring Nanny's commands to return to the nursery, Augustus ran downstairs. He pushed past Rogers who was carrying a tray up the stairs and shoved Louise to one side when he met her at the parlour door. In the conservatory he struggled with the bolt on the door but it came free under his constant pressure and he stepped through the door to the terrace outside. He paused for a moment between the pots of geraniums, his eyes scanning the lawn for Leggat, the gardener.

He caught sight of the old man, bending down in the shrubbery bushes. Augustus ran towards him, shouting out his name.

The old man raised himself and turned to see Master John running down the lawn, still in his school uniform, his sandy-coloured hair flying about his ears. He pushed his cap back on his head and scratched his forehead.

'Leggat! Leggat!' shouted Augustus as he drew near. 'You have to help me find my sister.'

'Well, now, Master John,' said the

old man, reaching inside his breast pocket for his pipe, 'I don't know if I can do that.'

'Yes, you can,' said Augustus, 'she came from the cabbage patch, Nanny said so.'

The old man looked straight at Augustus. 'It's not for me to tell you something different from Nanny, but I do know that you won't find that baby girl there.'

'Well, where is she?' Augustus said, the tears threatening to emerge again. 'I want to see her.'

Leggat picked up his bucket with the weeds inside and walked off. Augustus followed him. The old man stopped at for the orchard. He pointed at two of the largest apple trees.

'You see those trees, Master John?'

The boy nodded.

'Well, think of them as being a Mama tree and a Papa tree. Just behind them is another tree, do you see that, let's call that tree Augustus. And you see this tree here, this little one with the brown leaves? Well, this is a sick tree and very soon it's going to die. It's not a very strong tree and it can't support itself in the winter with all the rains and winds. We'll call it a "Jacqueline" tree.' He glanced at the boy who was staring blindly at the tree.

He continued. 'Now, when the Jacqueline tree dies, the other trees are going to be very sad for a while. They will miss her, the Mama tree, the Papa tree, and even the Augustus tree. But you know, it might not be very long before there's *another* tree here in this orchard.'

'Another Jacqueline tree?' Augustus looked up at Leggat.

'Maybe, maybe.' The old man shook his head. 'Or maybe it will have another name. A boy's name, perhaps. The other trees will remember Jacqueline, but they will like the new tree and want to keep him – or her,' he added hastily.

Later that afternoon, Augustus looked out from the nursery window. Dusk was falling but he could see down the lawn to the orchard. The wind had picked up and the branches of the trees were blowing into each other. There they were, the Mama tree, the Papa tree and the Augustus tree. There was a space where the little tree with the brown leaves had stood. The ground had been freshly dug over and Leggat's spade was standing upright in the earth.

'Goodnight,' whispered Augustus so that Nanny wouldn't hear him. He blew a kiss. 'Goodnight, Jacqueline.'

All children require playtimes: they will work all the better for it. Forced intellects are like forced fruits and flowers, insipid and imperfect. Fresh air and sunshine give us the fairest flowers and the finest fruit. It is the same in the growth and development of our children.

*The Lady*, 19 March 1885

# NEW LIFE

# Bringing up Baby

IF the mother-to-be walks into any good bookshop today it is more than likely that she will find a wide selection of books about pregnancy, baby-care, motherhood and child-rearing. With either Spock, Leach, Kitzinger or Brazelton in hand she will be able to find the answer to almost any question on 'babyhood' and she can bring up her baby by one book, or all four if she so chooses. This was not the case three hundred years ago. John Locke's *Some Thoughts Concerning Education*, which was written originally as letters to a friend, was first published in 1692 but it must have been read only by the upper classes, who had the ability to do so, and could not have been widely circulated by today's standards.

As far as child-rearing practices are concerned, the eighteenth century was the dawn of enlightenment. It was during this century that people began to address the serious problem of infanticide and to deal, if in a small way, with the large numbers of orphans who were left on doorsteps in every city and town. The English were considered by some people to be the worst culprits in neglecting their offspring, preferring instead their horses and their dogs. An anonymous eighteenth-century writer complained of the fact that in England there were more books on farriery than raising children. But as the public conscience awoke to the plight of infants, so books and pamphlets began to appear on the subject of infancy and the role of mothers. By and large, most were designed to be read by doctors, midwives and foster mothers, but very soon the writers realized that a market existed amongst new parents who were ready to question the age-old methods and hand-me-down ideas.

Most writers understood that their knowledge was limited, but nonetheless

Augusta, Princess of
Wales, with her
Household, *including*
*the young Princess*
*Augusta, seated on he*
*knee, by Jean-Baptist*
*Vanloo (1684–1745)*

## THE PRAM HOOD AND COVER

*'Do you advise putting baby outside in the garden in wet weather with the hood up? I find the waterproof cover causes the blankets underneath to become quite wet from lack of ventilation. On the other hand, I have understood that a baby should be put out in all weathers, except fog.' (Age, 5 months.)*

I wonder if it would be possible for you to put baby's pram in a porch or some such shelter when it is raining? This is healthier than having to put the hood up and the waterproof cover on. As you say, this certainly prevents free ventilation and the blankets become damp. If this is impossible I suggest that instead of putting baby outside you put the cot or pram in a room beside a wide open window. The pram hood and cover should only be used in a case of emergency.

'Letters About Baby', Sister Morrison (SRN, CMB, MTS), *The Nursery World*, 15 January 1936

this did not prevent them from advocating strongly certain methods and practices that we would today find most unappealing. Several of the writers were men who believed that they knew far more about babies than any woman, and since women were not generally highly regarded, they argued, how could it be that a woman would know very much about children?

In the 1740s several books were published on paediatrics, including one well known partly because it was written in English instead of Latin, William Cadogan's *Essay on Nursing and Management of Children*, which was published in 1748. Five editions of his essay were printed within three years. One of the most popular books of the eighteenth century was *Emile*, published in 1762, written by Jean Jacques Rousseau, whose own children were reportedly placed in a foundling hospital.

In the nineteenth century more and more people, both men and women, turned their attention to child-rearing, but some of the notions seem to us today to be so absurd as to belong to the ideas of an earlier, less well-informed century. Mrs Isabella Beeton, for example, in the mid-nineteenth century firmly believed that large groups of adults should not be permitted to spend time with a baby as babies required a great deal of oxygen, and the carbonic acid and mephitic gas that adults gave off through their skins was harmful to infants.

Child-care literature in the form of almanacs, pamphlets, books, magazines and papers became immensely popular in Europe and America from the 1800s. In 1803 Dr William Buchan wrote *Advice for Mothers*, and in 1832 *Mother's Magazine* was first published, followed by *The Mother's Assistant* in 1841. 1854 saw the publication of a popular book *Young Wife's Guide During Pregnancy and Childbirth*. Some magazines lasted only a few issues, others were more successful. *Parents' Magazine* ran from 1840 to 1850. *Baby, The Mother's Magazine* appeared in 1889, followed by *Babyhood, The Mother's Nursery Guide*, in 1891. In 1925 *The Nursery World* was published. Designed to be read by both mother and nurse it contained articles, which must have been helpful to a minority at the time, on subjects such as 'The Child in the Servantless Home', and it offered advice 'over the tea cups' on varied topics from suitable cot trimmings, nursery decor, the preparation of a sick room and the role of father; while Sister Morrison dispatched diet sheets and weaning tables to eager readers. The magazine, which has changed considerably since its first appearance, is still being published today.

The Hatch Family *of New York with their eleven children, painted by Eastman Johnson*

During the nineteenth century the mother became the focus of this literature, being credited with an increasingly important role. By the turn of the century writers were considering the concept of babies as individuals, with their own distinct personalities. In 1938 Anderson and Mary Aldrich wrote a book, the title of which, *Babies are Human Beings*, perhaps expresses better than anything the sentiment of the decade. Less than ten years later the work of Dr Benjamin Spock became known to the world, and since that time library shelves have been increasingly well stocked with volumes on every aspect of pregnancy, motherhood and child-raising.

163

The early paediatric writers of the eighteenth century first attacked the practice of swaddling babies. Cadogan's voice was one of the loudest on this subject. He believed that clothing should be loose and changed daily. He also advocated daily baths, but it was Locke who suggested that infants might benefit from frequent *cold* baths.

The wearing of wool was widely advised in the late nineteenth century and details were given as to how many layers of clothing should be put under, or on top of the woollen garment.

On the subject of feeding, most writers felt that infants would benefit from being breast-fed, rather than being fed with a gruel mixture, which the writers felt might be potentially dangerous. Some deplored the use of substances which calmed a crying or agitated baby such as gin, beer, or opium in the form of Godfrey's Cordial, 'Quietness', which was a boiled-down extract of poppy seeds, and laudanum which many wet nurses smeared on their nipples in the hopes of putting the baby to sleep.

The following piece of advice is fairly typical of what the new mother might expect to find between the pages of a home manual or book on child-raising in the nineteenth century. *The Complete Home*, which was written by Mrs Julia McNair Wright in 1879 and published in Philadelphia, advised women to be sensible on the subject of feeding and allow a child of six months of age a 'clear mutton broth or beef tea'. By the time the child was almost one year it was thought appropriate to give him or her some broiled beefsteak or a wing of fowl.

Cures for various ailments associated with babies make shocking reading. Leeches were commonly used in the medicine of the past and doctors did not hesitate to prescribe their use for babies. They were used for convulsions, for catarrh, when a leech was put on the baby's nose, and for croup, when one was put on the windpipe. Herb infusions were widely administered, along with rhubarb, calomel (mercurous chloride), suppositories and castor oil biscuits. Smallpox inoculations were introduced in the eighteenth century but it wasn't until 1891 that an anti-toxin for diphtheria was discovered, and it was 1907 before meningitis could be cured.

Teething babies were purged or bled. Their gums were rubbed with fresh butter, milk from a bitch or brains of a sheep. Sometimes they had their gums lanced, and most often they were given gin to drink or a few drops of laudanum. As babies were often sewn into their nappies, many suffered from

nappy rash and the old-fashioned cure for this was rainwater or powdered zinc.

Unlike today when we actively encourage and indulge in childhood, babies in the past were not allowed to be infants for long. Once swaddling bands were no longer worn, babies required more attention. Boys wore petticoats so that they could urinate on the ground beneath them, but in many cases infants were toilet trained, for whatever passed as the toilet, as fast as possible to cut down on the washing and changing, and many youngsters were out of nappies by the age of one year. Few potties exist but it is generally assumed that some sort of chamber pot was kept handy for household emergencies.

Much of the literature took the role of mothers and nurses to task. Mother was encouraged to feed, wash, dress and undress the baby herself, but to let the nurse amuse the child and carry out a great deal of the instruction. Nurses were warned of the potential damage to the brain created by bouncing babies in their prams over rough ground. Crawling was not approved of in the nineteenth century as crawling infants reminded people of animals, so babies were put into walkers as soon as possible. Rocking cradles went out of fashion in the nineteenth century, as many people thought the rocking action capable of creating damage to the infant's internal organs. Cuddling was frowned upon at this time, as was kissing, to which there were serious objections as described in a book *Care and Feeding of Children*: 'Tuberculosis, diphtheria, syphilis and many other grave diseases may be communicated in this way. Infants should be kissed, if at all, upon the cheek or forehead, but the less even of this the better.' The popularity of the pram, which automatically distanced the child from its parent or caretaker, must have pleased some writers.

There were many discussions over how long and how often the child should be allowed to sleep. People argued about whether babies should be left sleeping or woken up to be presented when visitors arrived at the house. During the nineteenth century mothers worried about whether baby should have a night light or not, and how many hours father should be permitted to spend with his son or daughter. The role of father was seen largely as that of getting the infant used to male company in general rather than encouraging any more intimate relationship.

Fathers have made only walk-on appearances in the social history of babies until fairly recently. One exception to this is the Eskimo father who helps to deliver the baby. In the last century fathers rarely visited the nursery and they are portrayed in literature as being awkward with babies and stern and strict with young children. However, it would be foolish to assume that all men fitted the ideas we have about them; certainly, in aristocratic households some men were known to have attended the birth of their children. These incidences took place, more likely than not, in an emergency and fathers were not encouraged, as they are today, to participate actively in the birthing process. By the turn of the century fathers were starting to play a different role and very soon there were special evening classes and discussion sessions for father to attend and books for him to read.

If people were starting to take due care of the physical needs of infants, it took much longer for their psychological welfare to be considered. The publication of Darwin's *Origin of Species* got people thinking and they turned their focus to the smallest human being, the baby. Until this time, some people viewed children as being the product of sin and therefore evil. Babies were believed to be born with the thoughts of the devil and the only way to drive the evil from the infant was with discipline. Many infants were whipped before they were ten months old and they were referred to as being 'broken', rather as horses are broken in before they can be ridden. Other children received an education which emphasized religious instruction and punishment, so that the child's parents could feel more secure about keeping the evil at bay. In complete contrast to this are the ideas of several African tribes, who believe that babies are gifts from the gods, which goes a long way towards explaining what appears to us to be a lack of discipline and training in youngsters.

Some Victorians viewed their children rather as greenhouse plants which the parents, as gardeners, were required to nurture. Like plants, or even animals, these infants were seen as uncontrollable and unruly, yet vulnerable and fragile. Others felt that the baby was a complete blank when it was born, devoid of personality, and that its parents were responsible entirely for forming its character.

The baby in the middle- and upper-class family was isolated to a great extent. Houses were large and built on several floors, so the nursery was cut off from the rest of the house. Things changed, of course, after the First

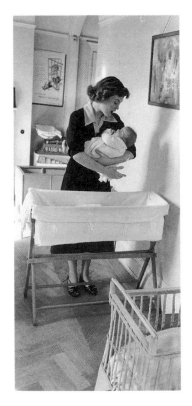

*In 1954* Picture Post *threw light on the problem of the unmarried mother and her child with a visit to one of the homes run by the London Diocesan Council for Moral Welfare Work*

World War and again after the Second World War, when the class structure was altered for ever and houses became smaller and surroundings more intimate. From what it is possible to glean from the last century, it seems that babies were left much to their own devices. In a poor household no one had time to play with the baby, but on the other hand a baby living amongst children and adults might well have received more attention than a single child in a wealthy home with only Nanny or 'Nursie' to fuss over them, when the latter wasn't busy attending to all the day-to-day details of running a nursery.

Few cot toys exist, so historians have drawn the conclusion that few were made for the baby. Certainly toys were used by older children and toddlers, but the mobiles and elaborate cot toys that are easily available today were unthinkable to earlier generations. So the baby was left to amuse itself, which he or she quite often did, to the horror of both nurse and mother. To the Victorians genital stimulation was the worst sin of all, and the curious infant would have his or her hands tied to the cradle posts, or their hands would be encased in metal mittens designed for this purpose. Thumb-sucking was another sin and in a publication of the US Children's Bureau a 'cuff' was recommended which was designed to keep the child's arm completely stiff. The smaller cuffs, which encased the fist, were worn well into this century.

If the baby cried, people thought it was exercising its lungs, although some felt that crying should not be allowed at all. It wasn't until this century that people really wondered why babies cried and it was Spock who suggested that babies who cried after they were fed and changed were doing so because they were tired or bored. Spock's book *Baby and Child Care* has been translated in almost thirty languages and sold over twenty-six million copies. His effect on several generations of babies is enormous, as anyone familiar with his work can testify.

In this century we have occupied ourselves with such subjects as feeding schedules, stimulating interest in our offspring, suitable playtimes and play toys, how close or how far to place these toys next to the baby, whether or not one should give the baby a rattle, how to avoid spoiling a baby, methods of toilet training, and bathwater temperatures and times. Private and government money is available to researchers for the study of infant behaviour. The more ambitious parents try to teach their children a second language while the infants are trying to master a few words of what will be their first.

## THE PERFECT BABY

It sat seraphic in its pram,
It never smeared its face with
   jam;
It kept its rattle clean and bright,
It never squalled, except at night.
It never roused paternal ire
By falling backwards in the fire,
Or licked the paintwork off the
   doors,
Or squashed blackbeetles on the
   floors.
It never sulked and never cried,
Remained austere and dignified
When called a lot of silly names
By fat and tactless Uncle James.
It loved its bath, and when
   immersed
It never howled, or kicked, or
   cursed;
Nor added to its nurse's toil
By jibbing at its castor oil.
In fact, it dawned upon me
   rather,
It wasn't in the least like Father!

From *Books of Today and Tomorrow*,
quoted in *The Nursery World*,
2 December 1925

Children in the past, rarely infants, were encouraged to read, but no children's literature existed until the seventeenth century and until that time the child would have been expected to learn words from the Bible. Most of the classic children's literature was not written until the nineteenth century. Early books for babies were made up of pictures, cut from adult magazines, which were pasted on to muslin sheets and then sewn inside a card cover. Today, word cards are strung up in baby's cot so that he or she can get used to the sight of the printed word, quite literally, from birth.

Today it appears, if one judges from the books available, that we are all-consumed by the subject of parenting. Many of the books deal with the potential guilt parents might feel if either they, or their offspring, fail to keep up with what are considered to be the landmarks in child-rearing. Many books deal with an analysis of what kind of parent the reader thinks she is — something no parent in an earlier century would have considered — while others are more specialized, such as *The Woman Who Works, The Parent Who Cares*, and even the *Parent's Book of Toilet Training*. Parents are now thought to suffer from 'rattle fatigue', and they are encouraged to ask themselves whether or not they want to go through the child-raising business a second time. Articles discuss the ideal number of years between children, sibling rivalry and how to deal with children who were known as 'hyper-active', but are now thought of as being potential 'over-achievers'. Meanwhile, slick magazines offer parents all kinds of apparatus and nursery equipment which will enable them to keep up with the Joneses.

Today there is a very definite need for advice: with smaller families, grandmother or mother may not be on hand to offer help and encouragement. But while some of her ideas may be rejected, many are still found to be helpful because they are ideas that have passed the test of time.

# Nursery Life

EALTHY parents have always employed other people to look after their children. Royal children in the Middle Ages had a wet nurse, a 'dry' nurse and one or two 'rockers', young girls who were hired to take it in turns to rock the baby's cradle. The baby who would become Louis XIV had a cook, a laundress and two laundrymen, a doctor, two nurses, a wet nurse and a governess as well as several pages. Even today, if they can afford it, some parents hire tutors, nannies and even bodyguards, to look after their offspring; and the *au pair*, over the last twenty years, has become an acceptable alternative to nanny.

For a child to receive all this attention there must be a room, or set of rooms, in which he or she exists as a satellite to the main house where the rest of the family reside. The word 'nursery' can mean one room, or several, and the size of a nursery depends on the size of the house. The larger the house the greater the likelihood of there being a nursery wing with a day nursery, a night nursery where nanny would sleep with the children, a room for the nursery maids, a pantry, a parlour for when mother came to visit and even an adjoining schoolroom. In smaller homes the nursery was actually a day and night nursery, or a night nursery when the back parlour in the house became a day nursery for nanny and the children.

When we think of a nursery, a vision comes to mind of a pastel-shaded room containing scaled-down furniture and examples of the culture of nurture, such as feeding bottles, high-chairs, potties and toys. In large medieval homes there was a 'nurcerie' which we must assume was separated from the other rooms in the house, but given what we know of medieval

169

homes there were very few rooms anyway, so it may well have been that the 'nurcerie' doubled as another room.

The nursery we recognize today, with special furniture and toys, dates from the eighteenth century. The nurseries about which we have the most information date from the nineteenth century, largely because of nanny, who appears in our social history as a prominent figure between the 1840s until the Second World War. Perhaps the greatest change in the nursery from over the last hundred years or so is that nanny no longer rules supreme.

In the nineteenth century nanny was one of the most important figures in the home. She ruled the nursery, occupying herself with washing, dressing and feeding the children, taking the babies out in the pram to the park where she paraded them in front of other nannies and making sure that they were suitably dressed to present to grandmother when she came to visit.

According to the nineteenth-century view, children were born essentially evil and they would need to be corrected from the beginning if they were going to lead useful lives. Many parents trusted entirely the physical, psychological and moral welfare of their offspring to nanny, whose opinion might even be asked when it was time to select a school for the eldest son. An infant was deposited in a cradle until he began to walk, when he would be placed in a walker. Childhood was short, infancy even shorter, and children were forced into what we think of now as premature adulthood. Boys in particular were treated as children only to the age of seven.

It was nanny's responsibility to teach the children in her care to read a few words, say their prayers and mind their manners. She was expected to administer punishment, correct their posture and turn them into God-fearing citizens. Nanny encouraged her charges to be good and didn't hesitate to threaten hell if the children did not comply. While we know a great deal about nannies and the children they reared, due in part to literature, and to an excellent book on the subject, *The Rise and Fall of the British Nanny* by Jonathan Gathorne-Hardy, we know little about nannies and the infants for whom they cared. Adults remember early childhood, not infancy, and many memories of nanny come to us from children who were at least old enough to recall them.

In many cases nanny had more than one charge. Victorian families were large and it was not uncommon for a nursery to contain several children under five years of age. In a large nursery nanny would spend most of her

*An extraordinary tiled frieze in this
nursery at Cardiff Castle*

time keeping the toddlers occupied and organizing the nursery maids. Babies
were quite often left in cribs to amuse themselves.

The power available to nanny in the household resulted inevitably in
'nursery politics' with a hierarchy amongst the nursery staff within the
household staff, especially if the household was large. With the exception of
the kitchen staff the traditional female household staff consisted of head
nurses, upper nurses, nurses, under nurses, nursemaids, ladies' maids, under
ladies' maids, maids, parlour maids, and house maids, who were gradually
replaced over the years by nanny and one or two maids. Nanny did not do any
housework. That was the job of the maids.

Nanny wore a uniform which she needed to protect her clothing from
being ruined by a sickly baby, but this also served the purpose of reminding
people that she was in fact a servant. Invariably she wore a grey or blue dress
made of serge or silk alpaca with a stiff belt and starched white collars, cuffs,
apron and cap.

171

*Nurse*: On Lammas Eve at night
   shall she be fourteen.
That shall she; marry, I
   remember it well.
'Tis since the earthquake
   now eleven years,
And she was wean'd – I
   never shall forget it –
Of all the days of the year
   upon that day.
For I had then lain
   wormwood to my dug,
Sitting in the sun under the
   dovehouse wall.
My lord and you were then
   at Mantua –
Nay I do bear a brain. But
   as I said,
When it did taste the
   wormwood on the nipple
Of my dug and felt it bitter,
   pretty fool,
To see it tetchy and fall out
   with the dug.
   *Romeo and Juliet*, William
      Shakespeare

Governesses, by contrast, wore their own clothes and they were excluded from the household pecking order by their dress, their education and manner of speech. Unlike nanny who was often known by her surname, the governess was usually given a title. Governesses were often the daughters of wealthier families who had fallen on hard times and they had the unenviable position of being neither one of the servants nor a member of the family.

A potential nanny would join a large household at the age of twelve or thirteen as a maid in the nursery, helping nanny or one of the nurses. She would have had some experience bringing up her own younger brothers and sisters and if she showed a particular aptitude with children she could progress, over the years, to become 'nursie', as nineteenth-century nannies were known. By the 1860s nannies were in such demand that employment agencies specializing in placing nannies in households flourished. Nannies also advertised themselves in *The Times* or answered the situations wanted sections. A nanny taking up a position with a new family might be taken on six months' approval. If she was successful, her employment could continue for years with the same family, and she might even be called back into service after retirement if a grandchild appeared. A highly recommended nanny could travel from one family to another during her career, never long without a job. In some cases, she would take the name of the family she worked for, especially if it was a particularly aristocratic name, as this would put her in greater standing with her colleagues in the 'nanny hierarchy'. Overseas, the authority and bearing of the British nanny was greatly admired and many nannies found jobs both within the British Empire, as it existed at that time, and outside it.

Nannies were not all large, matronly figures, as Hollywood would have us believe. They came in all shapes and sizes and they were often the objects of great affection. Winston Churchill was particularly fond of his nanny, Mrs Everest, who died in 1895. He sent money regularly to a florist who was instructed to maintain her grave. English kings Henry V, Edward IV and Henry VIII provided their 'nurses' with annual incomes, and no doubt others in history have done the same. Some nannies became mother substitutes for the children whose parents were away for weeks at a time. Although children were not allowed to acknowledge the fact, many of them preferred their nanny to their mother who might be an infrequent visitor to the nursery. Nanny was the person who washed them, dressed them, kissed their wounds

better and tucked them in bed at night. When the time came to send a boy away to school, it was nanny, not his mother, that he clung to, and many boys wrote to their nannies from school far more intimate letters than they would write to their mothers.

Of course, some nannies were tyrants. They spanked their charges, locked them in closets and tied them to chairs. If parents knew what happened in the nursery they tended not to interfere and subscribed to the idea that 'nanny knows best'. After all, that was what they were paying her to do.

By the turn of the century nanny's reign was over and this certainly contributed to the demise of the nursery. Women wanted more demanding jobs with better pay, although nannies were not generally badly off as they were provided with clothes, food, accommodation and, depending on the generosity of the family, other expenses. But in the post-First-World-War years women had far greater choice of employment than ever before and few were interested in domestic service. Mothers, inadequate though they were made to feel, were finally being encouraged to look after their own children. Houses were smaller with less room space.

Nanny, while she was around, was often allowed an opinion when it came to furnishing the nursery. Many Victorians put a great deal of thought into the design of the rooms. Baron Stockmar, consulting physician to Queen Victoria, advised the royal couple that the nursery should have light, airy rooms with plenty of sunlight. Some parents took the fresh-air fad to an extreme and suspended their young on specially designed trays from an open window. Other parents instructed nanny to carry the baby about on a pillow or cushion in front of an open window so that the baby might benefit from fresh air. This was in complete contrast to the views of the previous century when fresh air was avoided at any cost.

While the 'experts', writers on baby-care in the nineteenth century, thought it appropriate to hang paintings or engravings on the walls, especially those with religious subjects, *The Nursery World*, in 1935, felt that framed pictures might harbour dust, and recommended cut-out pictures which could be pasted to the walls instead. Colour was something that most writers felt strongly about. In Victorian times green wallpaper was vigorously discouraged not, in fact, for the colour but because it was supposed to be coloured with arsenic of copper which was poisonous. Early twentieth-century writers thought that father might engage his skills in painting interesting designs on

*Victoria with her nurse, c. 1891*

*This nursery was in the home of Arthur T. and Ella L. Lyman, at 16 Mt Vernon Street, Boston, Massachusetts in the 1880s*

the lampshades, but colour was to be controlled: no bright outbursts, rather, soft muted tones suitable for a young child.

A few writers did not think it necessary to make the nursery safe by barring the windows or blocking the fireplaces. They felt that children should learn through obedience to avoid dangerous places. Special infant furniture was not necessary, it was believed, as by using adult furniture a child would more quickly leave childhood behind and become an adult. Other writers disagreed and insisted that it was better for the child to have his own set of furniture.

By and large, with the exception of high-chairs, cots and cribs, nursery furniture was made from pieces that existed in the home which had been cut down or adjusted to suit the scale of the nursery. By the 1870s special purpose-built nursery furniture was being sold and it met a ready market. Household favourites such as Windsor chairs were rescaled to infant

174

proportions. Craftsmen designed special wallpaper, paintings and rugs for the nursery with special china and tiles decorated with characters and images adults thought suitable for the nursery. Elaborate *pâpier maché* bath tubs were sold to replace the old tin models. Nursery screens covered in 'scraps' of images printed by chromolithography, the kind that are highly prized by antique dealers today, were used to keep out the draughts. Playpens appeared at this time, and they were advertised as being 'even better than a nurse', and infant gymnasiums or 'baby jumpers' were strung up from doorways. High-chairs, often designed with their own lift-out potties in the seat of the chair, became fixtures in the nursery, but the potties were permanently removed from the design in the early twentieth century. Anything French was viewed as being very much in vogue and far superior to anything English. The rocking chair was a fixture in many homes, not just in the nursery, but obviously as furniture for an adult rather than a child.

In the twentieth century more specialized furniture became available for the nursery, and especially for mother who was now bringing up baby by herself. Nappies, or diapers, developed from a triangle with hooks and eyes in the 1850s, then still known as a clout, or tailclout, to the contemporary

*Five leap-year babies were born at Queen Charlotte's Hospital in London in 1928*

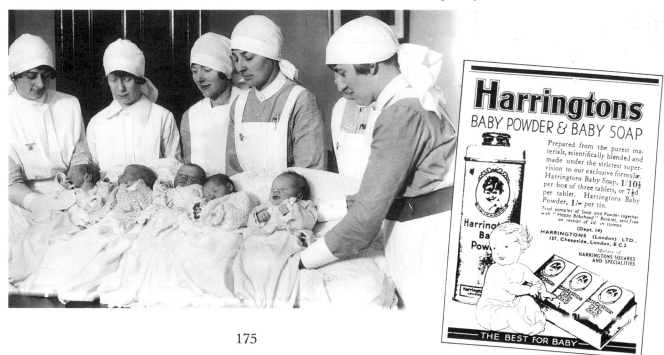

175

## HYGIENE

One of the most important and beneficial habits that can be taught a child in early life is to keep its mouth shut when sleeping, and indeed all times when eating or speaking. In regard to appearance alone, this is a habit well worth cultivating, for we are all of us aware of the ungraceful appearance presented by a person who habitually keeps the mouth open, and of the great improvement visible when the mouth is shut. But the matter is far more important than this. The true method of breathing is to breathe not through the mouth, but through the nostrils, provided as these are with a fine network of hairs which filter and cleanse the air which is to reach the lungs, and which also warms it on its passage. Moreover, it is well known that sleeping with the mouth shut is a very great security against miasma and affections of all kinds which are transmitted by the air – if indeed it be not an absolute preservative from them. Mothers should from the earliest infancy teach their children to close the mouth. When once the habit is acquired it will not easily be lost, and it may be acquired by those in middle life who will make a point of not going to sleep so long as the mouth remains open. *Keep your mouth shut.*

From *The Lady*, 19 March 1885

In the Creche *shows a baby's swing, a playpen and several cribs*

disposable nappies of today. While most mothers of the 1950s, on reflection, would gladly have traded the kind of washable cotton nappy used then with the disposables of today, there exists now a trend towards towelling nappies. Microphones came into use in the 1930s, so that mother could hear her baby as she moved about elsewhere in the house.

In the 1940s the new mother could find advertised in magazines intercoms, 'Heir-way' high-chair pads, 'Kantwet' mattresses and 'Doggyfix' plastic clips shaped like dogs' heads which held back the crib covers while baby slept. Variations of prams, carry cots, pushchairs or strollers appeared on the market and parents took a greater interest in the safety and design aspects of these items.

Over the years toys have changed a great deal. The word 'toy' means

something of little value, an ornament, or object of curiosity. As we use the word now, as a noun, the toy has taken on an educational value, as well as being enjoyable to the infant, but this is a relatively new concept in our history. Children have always made 'toys' for themselves out of scraps of household objects and they can become deeply attached to something a parent might find completely inappropriate.

Before the 1850s toys were largely hand-made and a surprisingly large number were exported from Germany to other parts of Europe. Made of metal, wood or leather, these toys were sold at market stalls and bazaars in the late eighteenth and early nineteenth centuries, along with 'fancy goods' and items we would usually associate with a mercer. A 'Toyman' was the name for a toyseller, who sold, from the 1850s, dolls, drums, kites, marbles, jumping jacks, hobby horses, carts, hoops, soldiers, skittles, trumpets, stuffed and carved animals and building bricks, which were thought of as educational toys. Most of these items were unsuitable for an infant and no one thought much about stimulating baby in his or her cot; unlike today when the importance of play is stressed and the infant has plastic bath books, toys that can be pulled, pushed and made to squeak, and bells that can be rung dangling in his cot, as well as coloured boards with letters or words inscribed upon them and, of course, a nest full of soft, cuddly toys, each one having passed stringent safety tests.

Rattles, of course, are one of the few infant toys that are still in use today, although they are very much changed. African infants are given a pod to play with in which several seeds rattle around inside, and no doubt wooden rattles were made for babies. If these items were poorly constructed they did not survive and the nursery relics today consist largely of baby walkers, cots, cradles, cribs and the elaborate silver rattles which were often given to infants as christening presents.

If the infant of the past had little to play with, then he or she might be lucky and have a nurse or nanny who was fond of music and nursery rhymes. Most nursery rhymes date from the sixteenth, seventeenth and eighteenth centuries, although some were adapted from medieval poems and ballads which were originally intended for adult ears only. It is to the nineteenth-century nanny that we owe a large debt, because it was nanny who kept those famous nursery rhymes alive over a hundred years or so and preserved them intact for us today.

THE NURSERY

There is nothing like toys for making a litter,' was the remark made to me once by a nurse, in a very significant tone. I had to acknowledge that children were rather given to leave their playthings lying about. Nevertheless, toys are very necessary to a child's life.

Every child should be early taught to amuse itself with its toys. One who requires to be constantly amused gives endless trouble. Some little ones have the happy knack of not only being able to amuse themselves, but of amusing others also.

Watch this child, and you will see that he will find occupations and interests for himself all through life. A close observer will notice even in the nursery many little traits that indicate the future character of the child. Every mother ought to be a close observer of her children from their earliest years, it will be of great assistance to her in their training.

Toys also are a help to education; they ought therefore to be both in good taste and true to Nature. From its earliest years accustom your child to like what is beautiful. To our eyes the toy soon becomes ugly and misshapen from the ill-usage it receives, but with the child the first impression remains; consequently that ought to be a good and right one.

From *The Lady*, 19 March 1885

# First Steps

INFANTS were encouraged to walk at a young age for several reasons. Ambulatory infants were far more useful to their parents if they were able to fetch and carry small objects, rather than have to be carried themselves. A non-ambulatory infant would need to be fed and taken to the toilet, whereas an infant who was encouraged to fend for himself, and even to be toilet trained at an early age, was an advantage for most parents. Even in the last century, if a family was not very well off the baby would wear the best clothes possible (just as parents in some European countries today like to keep their children plump as a sign of parental affluence) and in the days before washing machines, cleaning clothes was a far more complicated process than it is now. By keeping children upright, there was less chance of having to deal with dirty clothes. But perhaps the most significant reason to encourage early walking was the dislike, especially in the Victorian age, of seeing infants crawl as this reminded people of the human baby's resemblance to a small animal. Crawling was considered to be barbaric, and some books of the period emphasized that a child should learn to stand upright as quickly as possible. In any event, the long robes in which infants were dressed deterred any serious efforts at crawling.

There were a number of ways in which people trained infants to walk, the crudest form being a hollowed-out tree stump in which the baby was placed. The rigidity of the tree kept the infant upright. 'Walkers', as they were known, were used by both rich and poor, and in the houses of the latter they were often home-made. One early walker was designed so that the child stood in a circular hoop that was padded with leather and attached to a long pole.

The pole was fixed to an upright stand in the ground and the child would walk around and around the pole rather like an animal drawing water from a well.

The baby walker, sometimes known confusingly as a go-cart in the USA, has been in use since the sixteenth century and possibly even earlier. Many of the walkers dating from the sixteenth and seventeenth centuries appear to us to be evil-looking contraptions, rather like cages, and a far cry from the brightly coloured plastic walkers in use today. Seventeenth- and eighteenth-century walkers were made of wood, usually oak, which was painted different colours. The colours have been lost to us today but a number of these sturdy shapes have been preserved in museums.

Walkers were usually designed to be hexagonal in shape with castors or rollers on each of the six sides. Some walkers were quite elaborately carved, while others were far more rudimentary. The child was placed inside the walker where it learned to push itself around, aided by the castors or wheels. This was where the nursery came in useful as many of the early walkers were rather crudely constructed and they would have damaged any furniture with which they came into contact.

*A sixteenth-century family scene shows children in cots, in a walker and at mother's breast*

*A mid-nineteenth-century American patented baby jumper*

179

During the nineteenth century, these walkers became more refined and less clumsy-looking. It was during the second half of this century that the concept of the child as an individual with his own mind, rather than a product of evil whose sins must be driven away, or a plant in need of care, gradually took hold. Strange as it may seem to us, not much thought was given prior to this as to an infant's psychological or physical welfare. Both boys and girls were hampered by the long skirts they wore, seemingly endless layers of clothing and the idea that fresh air was dangerous. In the nineteenth century adults began to believe that infants might actually benefit from many of the things previously considered taboo.

Not many walkers exist from the nineteenth century but there is evidence of an alternative teaching aid: that of the baby jumper which became popular during the second half of the century. This was a harness-like contraption into which the infant was placed. It was then hung from a door or ceiling at a height which could just enable the infant to keep his or her feet on the ground. These baby jumpers, or swings as they were called, in fact immobilized the baby even further because he or she could travel only on the same spot.

As is the case with so many infant objects, relatively few exist today but it is feasible to imagine that other types of walkers were used. A simple cart with four wheels and a stiff handle to push performed just as well as a walker, and no doubt these were exactly the kinds of objects that were thrown out or chopped up for firewood when they had served their purpose.

Inside the nursery other apparatus provided exercise for little limbs. See-saws and rocking horses were thought suitable for older children but the nursery would need to be quite large to accommodate these toys. As children were allowed to become increasingly active, so it was necessary to change the design and length of their clothing, but it was the 1930s before infants were wearing 'play' clothes, and this, of course, coincided with the availability of man-made fibres which were far easier to wash and dry.

As the idea of a more active baby was accepted it was accompanied by the problem of what to do with a stimulated, energetic toddler. Playpens were the answer. By no means a nineteenth-century invention – there appears to have been some kind of 'pen' for an infant in the fifteenth century – playpens were nonetheless considered a great help to mother and in many cases were viewed as being preferable to a servant or nurse, who might infect the child with one

*Originally brightly painted seventeenth-century baby walkers were obvious forerunners to our twentieth-century models*

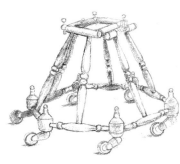

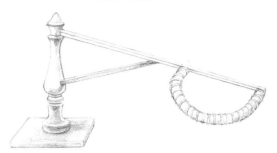

An early American baby walker. Placed inside the U-shaped area the infant would be required to walk around and around the centre pole

The modern Fischer-Price baby jumper with a seat

of the many diseases late Victorians thought the lower classes carried about with them.

In the twentieth century we still put our infants in playpens, out of harm's way, although now we go to great lengths to ensure that the pens are tested for safety, and we still encourage infants to walk, not because we dislike them crawling, although this may be the reason in some cases, but because we want to see our offspring progress. Many parents live in fear of having a 'backward' child, one who develops basic skills later than his or her contemporaries, so children are encouraged to walk as soon as possible. The basic difference between the baby walkers of the past and contemporary models is that modern walkers have seats. They are usually four-sided with rounded corners, four wheels, and they are painted with motifs. Some have headrests and trays in front which means that they can be used also as feeding tables as well as for the child to play upon. One version, sold in the United States, is made of decreasing sizes of inflatable rubber rings, obviously designed to protect the household furniture! Modern walkers are brightly coloured and made of plastic.

Baby jumpers or baby swings are still very much in use today but they are sold on the basis of being enormous fun for the infant, and at the same time, of course, they keep him or her off the floor and in one place.

# Going Out

O NCE an infant had been fed, washed and dressed in accordance with the customs of the time, it was time to go outside. From what we know of history, infants were carried about remarkably little until the nineteenth century. Of course, it was necessary to take them on journeys and there is some evidence that various carts were used in which to transport the younger members of families, but it is difficult to find examples of these vehicles and it is impossible to give an accurate representation of the ways in which children were carried about.

Tribal peoples have a simple solution to getting a baby from A to B. They simply wrap the infant in a cloth or carrier which they tie around themselves. The problem was more complex with the extraordinarily mobile society of the European Middle Ages when lords and their entourages of large households moved about from castle to manor all year round. A fourteenth-century manuscript reveals one way in which babies were carried, laid together in a large flat dish, which was then strung on two poles and slung over someone's shoulder. Babies must also have been carried in saddle bags, and one report records two horsemen suspending a cradle on two poles, the ends of which were attached to the horses' saddles.

Prams are relatively late inventions in our history, dating from the mid-nineteenth century, and early versions were described as child carriers, mail-carts and bassinets. Prams tell us a great deal about our culture. Prams evolved as a result of the change in attitude towards fresh air. Although a number of writers had recommended fresh air for infants, it wasn't until the nineteenth century that the idea began to be accepted, and, in many cases,

*This unusual baby buggy was designed by Gerrit Rietveld in 1918 but not made until much later*

there was still resistance to the benefits of fresh air in the early twentieth century. By placing a child in a pram we put a distance between ourselves and the baby, which evidently suited many Victorians who felt that proximity to the baby was most harmful. At the same time we are making ourselves, and the baby, more mobile, able to go to the store, to the park, to the beach.

The large old-fashioned perambulator which comes to mind when we think of the word 'pram' was introduced to England in the 1850s.

In 1846 Queen Victoria purchased three three-wheeled prams from Hitchings Baby Stores of Ludgate Hill, London, for a price of four guineas each. In 1853 Charles Burton was the first person to take out a patent on a pram. Burton had opened a shop in London's Regent Street in 1852 selling perambulators and shortly afterwards other stores opened. In the late nineteenth century many made their fortunes from the manufacture and sales of prams.

Early prams of the nineteenth century were the three-wheel kind in which the child sat with his or her back to the perambulator – the person who was doing the pushing – and, other than having only three wheels, one large one at the front and two smaller ones at the back, they were similar to the push chairs and strollers of today. These prams resembled invalid carriages which were also in use at the time.

*Perambulator.* One of the most useful inventions of the day . . . The great advantage of the perambulator is that it permits children to be out in the open without subjecting the nurse to any fatigue. It is as well, however, to lift the child out occasionally and to allow them to exercise their limbs until they feel tired when they can be placed in the perambulator again. In cold weather this is especially necessary as children being subjected to the exposure of the keen air in a state of inactivity are liable to be attacked with cramp, rheumatism and other painful affections.

*Dictionary of Daily Wants*, 1860

Promenade in Kensington Gardens *by John Strickland Goodall (b. 1908)*

183

THE WORLD OF THE BABY

*A baby carriage designed by William Kent c. 1730 for the Cavendish family. It was made to be pulled by a goat*

*The Ideal Landau*

Mail-carts, which were rather like prams, except that they were equipped with long extending handles which revealed their cart-like origins, were popular in the 1870s. In the following decade the bassinet came into vogue. This was a flat rectangular box made of basket-work which sat upon a chassis and resembled the pram that we think of today.

Towards the end of the century prams were seen just about everywhere and they were available to most people, although in order to use a pram in Berlin one would need a licence. The *Dictionary of Daily Wants* described the common practice of 'nursemaids to wheel their young charges to a certain spot, and to leave them sitting in their prams by the hour together, so that they may be spared the trouble of looking after them, and enjoy their gossip uninterrupted'. It went on to advise that 'Mother should put an end to this cruel practice by accompanying the children themselves as frequently as they can, or by making unexpected visits to the place where the children are taken.'

*Kensington Gardens in 1933, the fashionable deep-bellied prams out on parade*

*Every mother's dream of the 1950s, a Silver Cross baby carriage*

By the turn of the century the purchase of a pram had become quite a complicated matter. Manufacturers sold not only different types and colour schemes of chassis but varieties of springs, wheels, rims, fittings, handles and gears, not to mention a selection of fabrics and colours for the upholstery, the hood and co-ordinating sunshades. Prams became more colourful and stylish with names like the Cheltenham, the Torquay (Hitchings'), or the Totnes, the Paignton, the Romsey and the Pembroke (H. W. Twiggs & Co).

In the mid-1900s a number of 'collapsible cars', as they were known, became available, the Bethreena, for example, being advertised as 'All-British' and 'All Steel'. In one of these metal 'cars' baby could sit up or lie down and they were the forerunners of our modern-day pushchairs or strollers. The Atcars Company offered folding baby carriages for one or two children of polished birch or polished walnut.

The designs of prams varied over the years, often due to health reasons. In 1894 the average bed-length of a pram was twenty-six inches but by 1950 it was forty-four inches. The depth remained fairly constant, except during the 1920s when it doubled to about twelve inches, and this is one easy way in which to date prams from the period. Some historians have suggested the reason for this was that people felt infants would fall out of the more shallow prams. On a psychological level, the after-effects of war were good enough reasons for people to be extraordinarily protective of their offspring. During the 1930s medical advice was cited as the reason for larger but shallower

*Baby carriage available from 1902 Sears Roebuck catalogue*

*Silver Cross twin pram*

*Reed baby carriage*

prams. It was thought that germs might be harboured in the depths of these prams.

Prams in the 1930s had names such as the Hyde Park, the Dorchester, the Windsor, the Henley, the Princess and even the Duchess. Silver Cross and Brabingham were famous names in pram makers which were, until the 1920s at least, made by hand.

A number of more unusual prams appeared on the market in the 1920s: Dunkley's Pramotor which was a pram with a motor and one which attached behind. Mother stood on boards astride the wheel and steered the pram. Another pram of the period was designed to resemble a car with a chrome trim along the sides and even tail-lights. A pram from the Heywood-Wakefield Co., of Boston, Massachusetts, had red hub caps and a baby vision mirror. It was during the 1930s that the carry cot became popular. This was a cot which could be removed from the pram and used as a bed; the chassis would collapse in order to be folded into the boot of a car.

After the Second World War nannies were few and far between and it was now mother who pushed the pram not only to the park but to the shops. Smaller houses, closer living conditions and a general desire for lighter, more functional objects, that would fit in cars and down the aisles of a supermarket, made prams redundant in the 1950s, and by the following decade they were seldom seen. People preferred instead the new-style pushchairs and strollers which, over the years, became increasingly lightweight and attractive. In many an attic one can find a dusty old pram which, if the dust is scraped off, reveals a coat of paint in British racing green, a relic of a bygone age that was less than thirty years ago.

THE BARDS

My aged friend, Miss Wilkinson,
 Whose mother was a Lambe,
Saw Wordsworth once, and
 Coleridge, too
 One morning in her 'pram'.[1]

Birdlike the bards stooped over
 her
 Like fledgling in a nest;
And Wordsworth said, 'Thou
 harmless babe!'
 And Coleridge was impressed.

The pretty thing gazed up and
 smiled,
 And softly murmured, 'Coo!'
William was then aged sixty-four
 And Samuel sixty-two.

[1] This was a three wheeled vehicle
 Of iron and of wood;
It had a leather apron,
 But it hadn't any hood.

Walter de la Mare

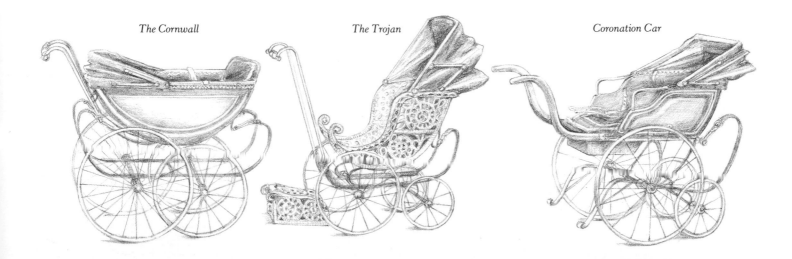

*The Cornwall*          *The Trojan*          *Coronation Car*

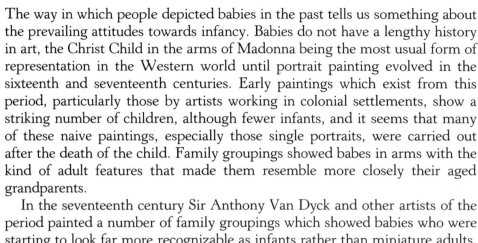

# Images of Babies

The way in which people depicted babies in the past tells us something about the prevailing attitudes towards infancy. Babies do not have a lengthy history in art, the Christ Child in the arms of Madonna being the most usual form of representation in the Western world until portrait painting evolved in the sixteenth and seventeenth centuries. Early paintings which exist from this period, particularly those by artists working in colonial settlements, show a striking number of children, although fewer infants, and it seems that many of these naive paintings, especially those single portraits, were carried out after the death of the child. Family groupings showed babes in arms with the kind of adult features that made them resemble more closely their aged grandparents.

In the seventeenth century Sir Anthony Van Dyck and other artists of the period painted a number of family groupings which showed babies who were starting to look far more recognizable as infants rather than miniature adults, despite their stiff poses which may, in fact, have had more to do with the restrictive swaddling bands being worn than any particular artistic device. An extraordinary work of art painted around 1645 by William Dobson, now at the Yale Center for British Art, shows a family group of mother, father and three children and in the top right-hand corner four skulls of what were presumably the deceased members of the family.

In the two decades prior to the French Revolution, the *maternité* portrait became fashionable. These were paintings, no doubt commissioned by wealthy fathers and husbands, of mothers holding their babies in their arms. The portraits are remarkable because one senses a definite bond, almost a tenderness, between mother and child which was previously absent.

But it was during the nineteenth century that babies started to appear regularly in paintings. Victorians raised large families, and the subjects of infant care and child-raising were starting to get a regular airing. It is not unexpected therefore to see babies in all kinds of Victorian paintings, either lost in mother's skirts in a mass of silk and lace in family groups, or the innocent party, in a cradle in a corner of a room, to a domestic drama.

Babies were painted at the beach, at the race track, on omnibuses, on street corners, in hay fields and even in pubs. More often than not, in the moralistic

*Not so much a baby but a cherubic version of an older child designed for a Victorian New Year card*

188

tones of the Victorian painters the presence of a baby tells a story of parental affluence, or approaching destitution.

These paintings, although they give us a great deal of information about the mobility, or otherwise, of the baby, about cots, carriages and cribs, about the clothing and the general culture of nurture, often appear to be overly romanticized and obsessive. During the Victorian era babies were subject to strange ideas. They were viewed either as evil and the product of sin, or as helpless, vulnerable human beings, totally ill-equipped to deal with the wicked world that awaited them. The sentiment that most artists chose to depict was that of devoted motherhood – appropriate for an age when mothers were being encouraged to take greater care of their children. One of the more curious customs of the nineteenth century was the habit of having a dead child photographed.

During Queen Victoria's reign photographic processes developed to the extent that small two-and-a-half-by-four-inch cards, known as *cartes-de-visite*, were produced in large numbers. In the 1860s miniature photographic portraits of the Queen, Prince Albert and the royal family were published and these became widely popular. It became fashionable for the new mother to have her photograph taken with the infant in order that a *carte-de-visite* could be made and distributed to her friends and relatives.

In the 1880s there was a vogue for sentimental pop-up cards, elaborately printed cards for St Valentine's Day, for Christmas, Easter and New Year's Day. Each one told a story in surroundings of lace and frills and lashings of violet and pink colours. Babies, ever popular subjects in the nineteenth century, were often featured on these cards.

In the twentieth century when cameras became available to the masses, it is rare to see a painting of a child. Instead, we can have instant pictures of the birth, and of the baby's every move until the grandparents are satisfied and at least one parent gets tired of taking film to be developed.

*Sepia photographs like this one were popular in the early twentieth century*

189

# Conclusions

There is no doubt that having a baby today is far different than it was in the past. Now it is much safer, both for mother and baby, and no longer is the sex of the medical practitioner an issue. In the 1980s Caesarean sections are performed routinely – almost too routinely, some women might say, who feel that the C-section has become a fashionable option. Premature infants can now live to lead perfectly ordinary lives. Even so, in spite of the giant steps taken by medical science, new parents continue to worry about SIDS (Sudden Infant Death Syndrome), and research continues into the use of fertility drugs and the incidence of births of mentally or physically handicapped children. Unlike in the past, today there are books available on just about every aspect of pregnancy, childbirth, infancy and the early years of child-rearing for fathers, mothers and even grandparents. A recent study in America estimated that by 1990 over $20 billion will be spent per year on baby-care products, baby clothes, books, furniture and accessories, with parents spending a third more on the first-born child than on any subsequent children.

Since the Second World War, a relatively short time in our history, a curious turn-around has taken place concerning childbirth. With the availability of effective contraception and changes in social attitudes, many women now choose to put their careers first and wait until they are in their thirties before they get pregnant. More often than not this results in smaller families and older parents. It appears that this trend will not change for the foreseeable future, and we are unable to foretell the effects of it on the family structure. It is early days to tell whether we make better parents if we have our children later; or to measure the effects of our children growing up in so-called 'nuclear' families, far removed from the Victorian situation where the older child helped bring up the younger siblings, and where grandmother was close at hand when advice was needed.

So, although one could argue that over hundreds of years little has changed in the practices of child-rearing, it now appears that, as we have children at different times in our lives, as we create babies *in vitro*, as fathers stay at home and look after the infants while mothers go out to work, we would like to start all over again and re-evaluate our roles as parents. The fact that we are looking for alternative ways of raising children than the manner in which we were brought up ourselves suggests a measure of dissatisfaction. It seems that we feel the need to consciously experiment with different child-rearing methods.

It will be the task of future generations to assess our progress. Did we make a 'better' job of being a parent than our own parents did of bringing us up? And did we therefore produce 'better' children? History teaches many lessons but it is unable to foretell the future.

# Acknowledgements

There were many people who helped me in different ways in the process of writing this book, and I should like to take the opportunity to thank them here. For assistance with my research most particularly I would like to thank Colleen Callahan at the Valentine Museum in Richmond, Va.; the staff in the Costume Department at the Museum of the City of New York; Jill Draper at the Edinburgh Museum of Childhood; Darrell D. Herring, Vesterheim; Ms. Avril Lansdell, Costume Curator at the Weybridge Museum, Surrey; Mrs N. A. Marshall, Bethnal Green Museum of Childhood; and Shelley Tobin at the Art Gallery and Museums and the Royal Pavilion, Brighton, Sussex. I would also like to thank Debbie Slattery of New Orleans, Louisiana, for her valuable points of view on the subject; at Michael Joseph, Susan Watt and Anne Askwith for being so organized and making so many good suggestions; my parents, Norman and Patricia O'Hara; and most of all, my husband, Steven Callan, who generously provided time and space for me to complete this book.

*Illustrations Credits: pages* 24, 49 (*Birth of St Edmund*), 51, 53, 68, 86, 93, 106 (*The Young Mother* by Hans von Bartels), 176, 179, Mary Evans Picture Library; 15, 57, 61, 65, 68, 75, 90, 103 (*The Mother's Darling* by J. Muller), 110, 125, 166, 173, 175 left, 185 left, BBC Hulton Picture Library; 1 (Victoria and Albert Museum), 9 (Towneley Hall Art Gallery and Museum), 81 (Musee des Beaux-Arts, Lille), 83 (Royal Holloway and Bedford New College, Egham, Surrey), 122 (York City Art Gallery), 123 (Roy Miles Fine Paintings, London), 141 (Christopher Wood Gallery, London), 152, *The Newborn Child* by Theodore Gerard (Galerie George, London), 183 (Christopher Wood Gallery, London, Copyright courtesy of Macmillan), 191, *The First, The Only One* by J. Haynes-Williams, all from the Bridgeman Art Gallery; 17, Andrew W. Mellon Collection, 100, Collection of Mr and Mrs Paul Mellon, National Gallery of Art, Washington; 32, 124, *The Illustrated London News Picture Library*; 30, reproduced by courtesy of the Trustees, the National Gallery London, 29, Copyright © 1947, The Metropolitan Museum of Art, Rogers Fund, 1947, New York; 163, Copyright © 1926 The Metropolitan Museum of Art, Gift of Frederic H. Hatch, 1926 (26.97); 42, The Mansell Collection; 39, Copyright © Christie's Colour Library; 44, The Thomas Coram Foundation for Children; 41, 115, Sotheby's; 58, 67, Kurt E. Schon Ltd, New Orleans, Louisiana; 74, 147, 149, courtesy of Dickins & Jones Ltd; 89, courtesy of Sotheby's Inc, New York; 87 right, Vesterheim, Norwegian-American Museum, Decorah, IA, USA; 82, Army & Navy Ltd; 84, 99, 128, 182, by courtesy of the board of trustees of the Victoria and Albert Museum; 113, Ferens Art Gallery: Hull City Museums and Art Galleries; 119, The Tate Gallery, London; 129, 184, reproduced by kind permission of the Chatsworth Settlement Trustees; 130, Tiffany & Co, New York; 133, 143, Bob Curtis/The Royal Pavilion, Art Gallery and Museums, Brighton; 134, Valentine Museum, Richmond, Virginia; 135, Sears, Roebuck & Co; 139, Weybridge Museum; 150 Smithsonian Institution, Washington; 144, reproduced by permission of Northampton Museums and Art Gallery; 145, 146, Musée de la Chaussure – Romans, France; 161, reproduced by gracious permission of Her Majesty the Queen; 165 above, courtesy of A & F Pears Ltd; 174, courtesy of the Society for the Preservation of New England Antiquities, Boston; 171, by courtesy of Cardiff City Council; 185 right, courtesy of Silver Cross; 188, courtesy of Celia Haddon; 117, Fine Art Photographic.